BFI TV Classics

BFI TV Classics is a series of books celebrating key individual television programmes and series. Television scholars, critics and novelists provide critical readings underpinned with careful research, alongside a personal response to the programme and a case for its 'classic' status.

Also Published:

Buffy the Vampire Slayer
Anne Billson

The Office
Ben Walters

Our Friends in the North
Michael Eaton

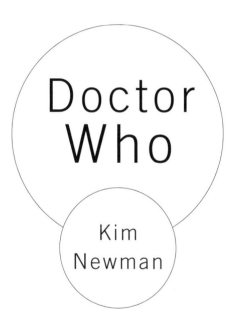

Doctor
Who

Kim
Newman

 Publishing

For Martin McKenna

First published in 2005 by the
British Film Institute
21 Stephen Street, London W1T 1LN

Copyright © Kim Newman 2005

The British Film Institute's purpose is to champion moving image culture in all its richness and diversity across the UK, for the benefit of as wide an audience as possible, and to create and encourage debate.

British Library Cataloguing-in-Publication Data
A catalogue record for this book is available from the British Library

ISBN 1–84457–090–8

Cover image: the Helix Nebula photographed by the Hubble Space Telescope (NASA, ESA, C.R. O'Dell (Vanderbilt University), M. Meixner and P. McCullough (STScI)).

Set by Fakenham Photosetting Ltd, Fakenham, Norfolk
Printed in the UK by Butler and Tanner Limited, Frome, Somerset

Contents

Acknowledgments

This book was commissioned by Rob White and brought to term by Rebecca Barden. Thanks for nit-picking, discussion and advice go to David Howe, Stephen Baxter, Paul McAuley, Steve Thrower, Dick Fiddy, Steen Schapiro and Paul Cornell; also, in various *Who*-related matters, my grandmother Miranda Wood, my parents Bryan and Julia Newman, my sister Sasha Newman and my nephew Jerome Newman.

Introduction

From 1963 to 1989, *Doctor Who* was a British TV institution. The first episode was broadcast just after dark, at 5.15 pm, on the 23 November 1963. The programme then settled into a Saturday teatime slot on BBC1, where it would remain for the greater part of its original run, most happily between *Grandstand* (1958–) and *Juke Box Jury* (1960). *Doctor Who* should not just be seen in the context of science-fiction television, lodged in history between Nigel Kneale's *Quatermass* (1957) serials and *Star Trek*.[1] The original scheduling was entirely apt: for decades, the show was a lively strand of mainstream British culture, watched by children and adults who had paid attention to the football results and would soon be thinking about the pop charts.[2]

The show began as mildly educational science fiction for children; its most obvious precedents were the *Pathfinders in Space* (1960–1) serials. Broadcast in the Sunday children's slot on ITV, *Target Luna* (1960) stretched to three sequels, taking schoolboy Jimmy Wedgwood (Michael Hammond), pet hamster Hamlet, boffin Dad (David Markham) and tagalong family to the moon, Mars and Venus. All were co-written by Malcolm Hulke – whose contribution to *Doctor Who* would include not only the turning-point 1969 serial 'The War Games' (which, among other things, introduced the Time Lords) but also the first book about the series, *The Making of Doctor Who* (1972). In his original brief, Sydney Newman, at the BBC as Head of Drama after supervising the *Pathfinders* serials at ABC, specifically excluded déclassé 'bug-eyed monsters' from the *Who* format. Newman, who first sketched the concept of the show, seemed to think the time-and-space-travelling adventurer hero should use a Wellsian time machine to visit past and future, learning about historical periods and solving problems involving 'proper' science.

Newman's big idea, presumably influenced by *The Incredible Shrinking Man* (1957), was a serial in which characters (through a never-repeated TARDIS malfunction) are reduced to insect-size and face peril in an ordinary garden. Writer C. E. Webber drafted 'The Giants', a story along these lines planned as the introductory serial, but it was rejected by the production team and cannibalised. Webber's first episode was completely transformed by writer Anthony Coburn into the pilot ('An Unearthly Child') that became the series' debut, leading into an entirely different adventure ('100,000 BC'), and the rest of the premise turned up in the second season opener 'Planet of Giants' (1964). Later, another production team solicited fresh ideas from the programme's creator and, apparently having forgotten 'Planet of Giants', Newman

Opening a door to the fourth dimension, William Hartnell

proposed the shrunk-in-a-garden idea all over again – it has since been reused in widely varying manners by Lindsay Gutteridge's novel, *Cold War in a Country Garden* (1971), the BBC science documentary series *Bellamy's Backyard Safari* (1981) and the film *Honey, I Shrunk the Kids* (1989). Though miniaturisation would turn up in a *Fantastic Voyage* (1966)-ish subplot in 'The Invisible Enemy' (1977) and more satisfyingly as the Master's favoured method of killing people, *Doctor Who* is not remembered as heavily dependent on such devices. In fact, the breakthrough to popular acceptance came with Newman's despised BEMs, who trundled on in archetypal form in the second serial, 'The Daleks' (aka 'The Mutants', 1963–4).

All lazy writing about *Doctor Who* trades on the stereotypes of children watching 'from behind the sofa' and studio sets wobbling. Both subjects are of some interest, but there is a lot more going on. The programme evolved into BBC-TV's most eccentric saga, at once cosily familiar and cosmically terrifying. When William Hartnell, the original star, couldn't carry on in the lead role, it occurred to someone that it had never been established that the Doctor, an alien, could *not* fall down one week and get up the next as a completely different person. This inspiration enabled the show to take on a characteristic of its hero and periodically regenerate, with recastings, upgrades (from black and white to colour) and reformattings (not all successful). *Who* originally see-sawed between British science fiction (epitomised in the 60s by John Wyndham, H. G. Wells and *Quatermass* – all sources at one time or another) and BBC period drama (a strong suit of the corporation's 'quality' tradition). Voracious for material, ideas and moods, the programme expanded to take in modes as variant as the surreal British trendiness of *The Avengers* (1961–9, another Sydney Newman idea developed beyond recognition by others), the blood-and-thunder gothicism of Hammer horror, panto humour, conspiracy thriller, studio-bound fantasia, social-satire comment, design-led futurism, deliberate *and* unintentional camp, even ambitious philosophising. This study follows *Doctor Who* (1963–89) from its beginnings – crucially the first episode, 'An Unearthly Child' (which

3

4

Travelling through time and relative dimensions in space

exists in two versions, showing major changes from pilot to
transmission) and 'The Daleks', which introduced the show's most
persistent and recognisable villains – through various regenerations of
lead actor, the comings and goings of secondary cast and monsters,
mushrooming popularity for at least its first fifteen years, decline into
niche cultdom (personally, I blame Mary Whitehouse, K9 and Douglas
Adams) and eventual cancellation, followed by the ghostly reappearance
of *Doctor Who* (1996), a one-off TV movie, and a happy ending in
Doctor Who (2005–), a fresh incarnation of the programme. I am well
aware of the two cinema films with Peter Cushing (and am especially
fond of *Daleks Invasion Earth 2150 AD*, 1966) and the *many* audio,
print, theatre and comic-book manifestations of the franchise but, for
the purposes of this book, they are non-canonical. It seems to me that

K9 – the shark-jumping moment?

Doctor Who was at its best and most interesting when addressing the widest audience (60s and 70s kids, plus their youngish parents) but lost its grip when it became aimed almost solely at its fans. I'm more interested in what made its many great periods great than in the problems that eventually undermined it – in 'jump the shark' terms, the show hopped on and off many times[3] – and even weaker periods produced *some* worthwhile stuff.

5

   The first television I can remember watching was *Doctor Who* (since you ask – 'World's End', Episode One of 'The Dalek Invasion of Earth', 21 November 1964). I stuck with the programme throughout the 60s, when it was essential kid-viewing – which means I saw the episodes now lost, and retain vivid impressions of 'The Evil of the Daleks' (1967), 'Fury from the Deep' (1968) and 'The Web of Fear' (1968) – and into the early 70s, when it seemed to grow up with its audience by becoming more ambitious in production and dramatic terms – with 'Doctor Who and the Silurians' (1970), 'Inferno' (1970) or 'Genesis of the Daleks' (1975), *Who* was no longer content to be a 'kiddie *Quatermass*'. I am of the generation that pestered parents to buy the first wave of merchandising: Dalek toys and badges, annuals, early novelisations and spin-offs, *Radio Times* specials. I can also confirm the authenticity of the

The Macra – seven-year-old Kim wouldn't go upstairs with the lights off after this episode

'behind the sofa' stereotype, that impulse to watch television which burned frightening images permanently into the mind. Few of the many horror films I've seen as a grown-up have terrified me in the way 'The Macra Terror' (1967) did when I was seven, and yet – for all the sleeping-with-the-hall-light-on business that annoyed my mother – it would have been unthinkable *not to watch*. I wavered as a devout viewer in the middle of Tom Baker's tenure and dropped out when K9 turned up (though I remained a casual viewer till the end). In recent years – thanks to cycled repeats on the UK Gold satellite channel and comprehensive video, audio and DVD releases — I have caught up with all the shows I missed on first broadcast, refreshed my memory of the serials I did see first time round (some bits of business or lines of dialogue remained lodged in my mind long after I'd forgotten what the Treaty of Utrecht was about or how an oxbow lake is formed) and come back several times to think about *Doctor Who*. In my other life as a fiction writer, I wrote a novella in a licensed spin-off line, *Time and Relative: The Diary of Susan Foreman* (Telos Publishing, 2001), that explored the beginnings of the first TARDIS crew.

BFI TV Classics: Doctor Who deals with its subject mostly chronologically, but I have tried not to get bogged down in giving 'equal time' to all periods of the show. Several players can compete to be reckoned the George Lazenby of *Doctor Who*, and entire seasons could pass without troubling the attention of any but connoisseurs of outdated fashions, hurried production methods or baggy rubber-suit monsters. I concede this opinion may have much to do with my age and that all eras of the show put out weak serials and classics, but from 1963 to K9, *Doctor Who* was important and from 1977 to 1989 it wasn't. In 2005, bizarrely, it's important again, which has meant a redrafting of the entire text shortly after the broadcast of what we must now consider Season One of a different but related programme. Though the subject of this book is the original, the newest incarnation – at the time of writing, on the point of mutating again with a Tenth Doctor (David Tennant) – inevitably commands attention. Sometimes, *Doctor Who* (2005–) is fascinating for the way it comments on its predecessors in a manner which suggests writer–producer Russell T. Davies is mounting a critical project as much as refreshing a still-potent concept to suit the demands of twenty-first century television. It is as if every Davies-stamped episode feels obliged to work in some bit of business that the old show should have got to years earlier but somehow overlooked. Deeply engaged with its previous incarnation, it can still stand as a working definition of a useful, creeping prefix by being 'not your father's *Doctor Who*'. It was inevitable that *Who* would be back, but that a new series would be a critical and ratings success was far less of a certainty.

7

Several excellent books have concentrated on the minutiae of the production, the in-house politics of getting the show made and simple essentials like listing all the credited and uncredited cast and crew. New readers should consult the following, though there is inevitable overlap (and equally inevitable dissent) and they represent the barest scratch at any bibliography: Doctor Who: *The Sixties,* Doctor Who: *The Seventies* and Doctor Who: *The Eighties*, by David J. Howe, Mark Stammers and Stephen James Walker (authors also of seven volumes covering regenerations of character and show, beginning with Doctor Who: *The Handbook: The First Doctor*); *The Television Companion: The Unofficial and Unauthorised Guide to* Doctor Who, by David J. Howe and Stephen James Walker; Doctor Who: *Programme Guide*, by Jean-Marc Lofficier; Doctor Who: *The DisContinuity Guide*, by Paul Cornell, Martin Day and Keith Topping; and *Who's Next: An*

Unofficial and Unauthorised Guide to Doctor Who, by Mark Clapham, Eddie Robson and Jim Smith. Also, a word for Mark Campbell's slim *Pocket Essentials*: Doctor Who – which has dates and credits in convenient form for quick reference. All these will doubtless continue to be reissued in updated form and several competing, authorised or unauthorised books about the latest regeneration have already appeared. Another useful item is the CD *Who Is* Dr Who (RPM), a collection of *Doctor Who*-related novelty pop – including 'I'm Gonna Spend My Christmas with a Dalek' by the Go Go's and 'Dance of the Daleks' by Jack Dorsey and His Orchestra.

Here, I'm more interested in *Doctor Who* as cultural phenomenon, reflection of its changing times and television masterpiece.

1 Relative Dimension

'An Unearthly Child' (1963), the first episode of *Doctor Who*,[4] is constructed as a mystery – 'who *is* the Doctor?' This is *partially* solved in twenty-five minutes, then dropped until 'The War Games' (1969) and periodically revisited and revised throughout the series' run.

The tone is set by the titles sequence, which combines monochrome video distortion with music from Ron Grainer and the BBC Radiophonic Workshop. Later regenerations added colour, the faces of the current stars or unfortunate semi-disco arrangements, but the first, simplest and strangest take remains the most evocative. The titles sequence was a mini-artform of the 1960s, with the development of opticals more complex than scrolling credits and even unmemorable programmes inspiring tunes that stick in the mind for decades. Composer Grainer and Workshop producer Delia Derbyshire broke with the British science-fiction television tradition of orchestral samples (*Quatermass* used snatches of Holst) and created a *Doctor Who* theme as catchy, experimental and indefinably weird as the work of Marius Constant for *The Twilight Zone* (1959–64) and Dominic Frontière for *One Step Beyond* (1959–61) and *The Outer Limits* (1963–5). Those waves of literal white noise – 'sound on vision' says a pub bore as ancient Martian evil disrupts the airwaves in *Quatermass and the Pit* (1959) – break with normal programmeming, a visual representation of 'up ahead, *The Twilight Zone*' or 'from the inner mind to . . . *The Outer Limits*'. A frequent signifier of the cosily unusual in 1960s television is an assurance that what is being transmitted may look like a fault but is, in fact, intentional. Picking up from the Control Voice ('there is nothing wrong with your television set') of *The Outer Limits*, a surreal children's comedy show was entitled *Do Not Adjust Your Set* (1967–9).

The show begins in a nondescript, foggy London street, in the middle of the night, with a policeman poking around. A large sign on some gates reads: 'I. M. FOREMAN – Scrap Merchants – Totter's Lane'. Since the Doctor's granddaughter calls herself Susan Foreman, it is briefly assumed that he *is* I. M. Foreman.[5] The circumstance is reminiscent of Winnie-the-Pooh living under the name 'Sanders', 'which means he had the name over the door in gold letters and lived under it'. The show's title is justified by two dialogue exchanges in the second episode, 'The Cave of Skulls'. Ian (William Russell) tries to address 'Dr Foreman', and the Doctor (William Hartnell) snorts 'Eh? Doctor who? What's he talking about?' Later, Barbara (Jacqueline Hill) similarly refers to Susan's grandfather as 'Dr Foreman' and Ian, who has paid attention, says 'That's not his name. Who is he? Doctor who? Perhaps if we knew his name we might have a clue to all this?' Though it lacks a question mark (in the early days, print sources often added one), the title is not a name but a question. The much-derided question marks that dot the costumes of later Doctors make up for the grammatical omission, but Ian's musing that the Doctor's secret name ('Rumplestiltskin'?) was an important clue would rarely be considered again. The makers of the Peter Cushing films and creatives behind early strips in *TV Comic* failed to realise that Doctor Who was not the Doctor's name; decades on, the title is just the title, worked into 'Rose' (2005) as a website (with question mark) and restated several times in the subsequent episodes as fed-up supporting characters echo Ian with a muttered 'Doctor who?'. Two lines (one mumbled and easy to miss) from 1963 are as rarely remembered as the reasons why the hardly skeletal Nick Charles (William Powell) came to be tagged the Thin Man or there were no filing cabinets in Jim Rockford's trailer.[6] Similarly, the early decision to list the character name as 'Dr. Who' in the end credits (and the *Radio Times*) remained until 1982, when he formally became 'the Doctor'.

The policeman passes, but we – the camera – glide into the scrap merchant's yard to discover, tucked away in a corner, a police box. As dialogue later points out, the siting is odd: to be any use, the box ought to be on a public thoroughfare. The familiar shape is at least appropriate to the general urban setting and (now-historical) period. The TARDIS turns up in far more unlikely landscapes, not excluding contemporary Britain of the 1970s and beyond when the original boxes – already semi-obsolete in the mid-60s thanks to changes in police communications central to another long-running BBC-TV series of this vintage, Z-Cars (1962–78) – disappeared almost completely. In a case of fiction eclipsing reality, the TARDIS displaces more cultural water than any genuine police box glimpsed in archive footage or a film like The Blue Lamp (1950), as if C. S. Lewis were so widely read that all wardrobes were seen primarily as portals to Narnia. On screen before the Doctor, his companions, the Daleks, the sonic screwdriver or even the title of the first episode, the TARDIS is the only constant in the show – which is ironic in that the machine is supposed to change shape to match wherever it happens to materialise but gets stuck as a police box when the 'camouflage unit' fails early in 'The Cave of Skulls'.[7] Boiled down to its simplest format, Doctor Who is a character actor and a police box. On its first appearance, the TARDIS gives off an electrical sound and 'feels alive' to the touch; though the interior would continue to thrum, these external signifiers of alienness would be phased out, until the TV movie and revival series decided that the time machine was practically a living thing.

Our way into the box, a doorway to the infinite, is through Barbara Wright and Ian Chesterton, teachers at Coal Hill School. From the lack of uniform, mix of boys and girls, the fact that Ian teaches Science and the frankly drab-sounding name, we take Coal Hill to be a secondary modern, which means alien genius Susan (Carole Ann Ford) failed her eleven plus exam or entered the British tripartite educational system without enough documentation to get into grammar school.[8] Though Coal Hill looks like a forerunner of Grange Hill (1978–), BBC-TV's comprehensive school-set soap, it was a television rarity in 1963, when children's programmes tended towards fantasy fee-paying schools, typified by Gerald Campion cadging buns in *Billy Bunter at Greyfriars* (1952–61) or Jimmy Edwards thwacking bottoms in *Whack-O* (1956-60). More savvy about its audience, *Doctor Who* expected viewers to dislike little toffs: Cyril (Peter Stephens), a sinister schoolboy dressed like Billy Bunter, is a hateful menace in an early serial, 'The Celestial Toymaker' (1966). Decades later, Romana (Lalla Ward) and Turlough (Mark Strickson), companions of the Doctor, would model St Trinian's or Greyfriars' uniform; that they (like Cyril) are obviously adults dressed up in fetish gear suggests a misty vision of British education – recently revived at Hogwarts – years away from credible, unlovely Coal Hill.

With a dress code progressive for its day and teachers committed enough to spot an alien in class, Coal Hill was nevertheless uniquely like the schools the bulk of *Doctor Who*'s young audience actually attended. These sequences anchor 'An Unearthly Child' in a reality from which the show could take off. It was typical of the well-intentioned, slightly bossy BBC of the early 1960s that our viewpoint characters should be *teachers*. If the series had been launched even a few years later, Barbara and Ian would have been fellow pupils. After the disbanding of the first team of regulars, the Doctor would rarely travel with companions as mature, sensible or generally well informed as this pair. The series' remit is even covered by their subjects: Barbara teaches History and Ian Science, which qualifies them to ask intelligent questions the Doctor snarls at impatiently. An interesting theme of the first serials is that, unlike Barbara and Ian, the Doctor is a *bad teacher*, a know-it-all who can't be bothered to explain or communicate with people not as gifted as he. Among other failings, dispensed with during his decades-long transformation into a dangerously perfect being, the Doctor has not taught his granddaughter how to cope with the year in which he has stuck her. Then again, he was against the whole idea of her going to school – so maybe he has pettishly let her make a fool of herself so he can be proved right, even if this does lead Ian and Barbara to the TARDIS and a forced flight into the unknown.

We first see Susan, who has a modish bob and an indefinable accent, listening to tinny pop music on a transistor radio which would have been instantly confiscated at my school. As Ian and Barbara discuss her unusual mix of aptitude and ignorance, we get flashback glimpses that show Susan as the laughing stock of her class. She doesn't know how many shillings there are in the pound because she has forgotten 'that the decimal system hasn't started yet' (one of the show's occasional smart guesses) and struggles with a maths problem because she wants to calculate in five dimensions (one of the show's frequent scientific fudges). She is obviously a misfit, and a fifteen-year-old whose only friends are *teachers* would risk being a Carrie-like playground pariah, but she later claims the months spent at Coal Hill have been 'the happiest of my life' – hinting at appalling elements of the backstory as completely avoided as the identity of her parents. While bouncing around time and space, often in uncomfortable or distressing circumstances, she never expresses a preference for getting back to double Geography on a wet Thursday afternoon. Susan is a paradox as a character, which might explain why she was rarely as well used as in 'An Unearthly Child'. She's an alien who has gone native, a teenage Thomas Jerome Newton who wants to be accepted as a real girl, but her plot function is to lead Ian and Barbara to the Doctor and, once that's over with, she is mostly used as a nuisance to string out a peril. In 'The Cave of Skulls', she launches herself like a wildcat at a caveman threatening her grandfather – but later episodes make her more timid (she is the first of *Doctor Who*'s many 'screamers'), though her odd statement that she likes walking through the dark ('it's mysterious') is put to the test in the next serial by a perilous night traipse through the petrified forests of Skaro that reduces her to hysterics.

There's talk of Susan's grandfather and presumed guardian, 'a doctor' who doesn't like strangers, but what really puzzles busybodies Ian and Barbara is the lack of an apparent residence at Susan's address. 76 Totter's Lane, appearing months before the similar main set of *Steptoe and Son* (1964–73), is a deliberately inauspicious, down-at-heel HQ for a putative adventure hero, as cluttered but a lot less classy than

13

The first TARDIS crew –
Barbara (Jacqueline Hill),
Ian (William Russell), the
Doctor (William Hartnell),
Susan (Carole Ann Ford)

Sherlock Holmes' digs in 221B Baker Street or Bruce Wayne's Batcave.
In 1963, a teenage girl might well have been ashamed to admit to
schoolfriends that she lived in a scrap merchant's yard – and she
certainly wouldn't want to own up to having a family in the rag-and-
bone business. The Doctor would depart from this grubby base and
never think of it again (at least not until 'Attack of the Cybermen',
1985), whereas Albert and Harold Steptoe (who had their own Ron
Grainer theme tune) would rarely venture beyond their enclosed,
rubbish-filled private trap. The junkyard is not a home, but a stopping-
off place; Susan and her grandfather live *inside the box*.

    The Doctor arrives after Ian and Barbara have trespassed in
the yard and found only the odd, humming police box. After years as a
film and TV gangster (*Brighton Rock*, 1947; *Hell Drivers*, 1957) or
NCO (*Carry on Sergeant*, 1959; *The Army Game*, 1957–61),
William Hartnell changed his image by playing the First Doctor with
long white hair, Victorian clothes and snorting, superior dialogue
delivery. 'An Unearthly Child' was taped twice, once as a pilot and
over again for transmission; between the two takes, Hartnell's
performance changes completely. At the first go-through, the Doctor
is rude, angry, dangerous and malevolent: Susan seems terrified of
him, which would give Ian and Barbara more cause to intervene, and
he transports the intruders to the remote past possibly with the intent
of kicking them out and stranding them there. This Doctor might

have been a continuing villain as much as a hero, an early alien abductor or a mean-spirited passenger in his own TARDIS, as prone to selfish or foolish acts that get his companions into danger (i.e. plots) as Dr Smith (Jonathan Harris) on *Lost in Space* (1965–8). An element of this reading remains in 'The Dead Planet', Episode One of 'The Daleks' (1963–4), where the Doctor underhandedly sabotages the TARDIS to detain his companions on Skaro – but he is motivated in this instance by curiosity rather than greed. The rethink between performances doesn't entirely eliminate the potentially dangerous, unsympathetic elements of the character: he is gruff, devious, smug and quixotic (and encourages Ian to touch an electrified switch), but he takes the trip into the past to teach the teachers a lesson, to prove the TARDIS can do what he says it does. Ambiguous characters were always possible in British adventure stories: the heroic Sherlock Holmes can be appallingly rude, the murderous Long John Silver is ingratiatingly daring.

    In *The Making of Doctor Who* (1972), Malcolm Hulke and Terrance Dicks set out (and perhaps embroider for young readers) the reasoning of Sydney Newman and Donald Wilson in envisioning the leading character in their new show. 'And what sort of man should he be? Tall, handsome, young, pleasant – the typical hero? No! "Let's make him a crotchety old man," said Sydney Newman, "at least 745 years old." ' Of course, the show covered its bets by including the tall, handsome, young and pleasant Ian in its initial set-up. By making the

15

A crotchety old man,
William Hartnell

Hartnell Doctor a crotchety old man, Newman and Wilson were perhaps thinking of a different archetype, not a hero but a hero's mentor, a holder of secret knowledge who issues wise counsel or sends a more hands-on adventurer off on quests and missions. The most obvious precedent is Merlin (a connection eventually laboured by 'Battlefield', 1989), but think also of Professor Xavier of the *X-Men* (another 1963 debut), Ian Fleming's M (or Q), Nero Wolfe (who sits with his orchids while Archie does the legwork), Van Helsing in *Dracula* or Dr Finlay's partner Dr Cameron. The Doctor wouldn't visit the nineteenth century until Patrick Troughton was kidnapped there in 'The Evil of the Daleks' (1967) and didn't truly blend in until Tom Baker pulled on a Holmesian deerstalker for 'The Talons of Weng-Chiang' (1977), but Hartnell's frock coat and Dickensian attitude make him seem a refugee from the world of Conan Doyle, gaslight, hansom cabs, imperial adventure and Jack the Ripper. This may have been a deliberate attempt to evoke the original time traveller, from the H. G. Wells' novel, and instils a certain steampunk sensibility into the entire *Doctor Who* canon. Subsequent Doctors have retained period fashion sense: shabby-genteel Troughton, dashing Pertwee (in colour, adding a scarlet lining to his ulster as Hammer's Dracula did to his cloak), Edwardian cricketer Davison, Wild Bill Hickock-costumed McGann.

Hearing Susan's voice inside the police box, Ian and Barbara brush aside the Doctor's objections and stumble in to find that (like the

Bigger inside than outside

wardrobe in *The Lion, the Witch and the Wardrobe*) the TARDIS is bigger inside than it is outside. The teachers are astonished. This moment will be repeated over and over, almost as a rite of passage for every regular on the show. It's such a mind-stretching concept that it has to be hashed over several times in clunky dialogue: 'You've discovered television, haven't you?' snips the Doctor, unhelpfully – reasoning that there is an equivalence between showing an enormous building on a small screen and the inside-out dimensions of his time–space machine. There are solid production reasons for the TARDIS's nature: the control room is a spacious, standing set (blinding white walls with signature roundels and the hexagonal central control console) while the police box is a moveable prop. At first, the interior seems to consist of this one room and the exterior might be an illusion: the doors open directly to the outside world and, seen from within the TARDIS, match the design of the control room, only taking the form of police box doors when looked at from the outside. Later, a few other areas would be seen – including back-up control rooms, like the wood-panelled version introduced in 'The Masque of Mandragora' (1976) when the production team got fed up with a hold-over set that had remained essentially a black-and-white design even after the show began to be made in colour. The possibility that the TARDIS's interior wasn't just bigger than the outside but *infinite* would be touched on from time to time but never quite take hold. The 1996 and 2005 revivals make the time machine a living, perhaps sentient thing with a habit of swallowing evil people whole and an energy source that might threaten any world the ship had stopped off on (invariably Earth) if mishandled (of course, this repetition could be down to Russell T. Davies cribbing the finale of 'Boom Town' from the last act of Matthew Jacobs' TV movie script).

At once a home and a ship, the TARDIS soon became cosy – though it breaks down often to suit the plot and prevent the Doctor from becoming too omnipotent a figure to be embroiled in various adventures. Originally, Susan states she invented the name, an acronym for 'Time and Relative Dimension in Space' (sometimes 'Dimensions'). The TARDIS is a utopian playroom, as opposed to the dystopian

17

playroom that would show up in 'The Celestial Toymaker'. It is as safe as being snug under the bedcovers, and similarly offers transport to dreams and nightmares. Occasionally, to demonstrate its essentially magical nature, the TARDIS would take the Doctor and companions not to another time or planet but to a limbo, dreamworld or alternative dimension, most successfully the 'Land of Fiction' in 'The Mind Robber' (1968). It is at once home base and vehicle, combining the functions of Marineville and Stingray or Tracy Island and the Thunderbirds; but, in contrast to the technophile kindergarten of Gerry Anderson's shows, there would be no schematics for the TARDIS, no blueprints to limit its dimensions. As a home, it isn't that practical – the control room has surprisingly few *chairs*, hence a great deal of standing around or falling about.

The TARDIS has that near-inviolability common to 221B or the Batcave: for a while, it seems the time machine only admits friendly folk, offering safe haven from any Daleks or cavemen who might be ranting and fuming outside its indestructible, impregnable shell. Even early on, the show is finding ways of using this sense of a reassuring home base to tighten the screws. At the end of 'The Survivors', Episode Two of 'The Daleks', Susan alone returns to the comfort of the TARDIS after a journey through the radioactive jungles of Skaro. She takes a moment to overcome her inclination to stay in this secure environment before forcing herself into the threatening world outside to save her companions. Most cliffhangers depend on climaxes of danger or revelation, but this is a rare instance of heroism as slingshot into next week's action. Frequently malfunctioning, a randomising element that serves to generate entire plots or more often to prevent too-easy escape from a story in progress, the TARDIS is nevertheless the show's safe house. Just as Dr Grimesby Roylott would explode into Holmes' rooms for shock effect in 'The Speckled Band', *Doctor Who* would eventually, if sparingly, have the TARDIS invaded by Cybermen or Sontarans to indicate more than ordinary peril. Originally, writers were cautioned against using the TARDIS too much as a plot device – it got the heroes to and from places, but did not solve their problems; Russell T. Davies would ignore this in 'The Parting of the Ways' (2005), in which the 'telepathic' vessel's conduit to the awesome forces of time and space is used to save the day, though at the cost of a lead actor.

The TARDIS's uniqueness would eventually be challenged: the Meddling Monk (Peter Butterworth) of 'The Time Meddler' (1965), the next member of the Doctor's as-yet unnamed race encountered, has his own, with a *working* chameleon circuit. It would be established that the Time Lords operate a fleet of the things (indeed, more advanced models) and several other rebel Time Lords (the Master, the Rani) have their own go-anywhere machines. 'The Edge of Destruction' (aka 'Inside the Spaceship', 1964), a two-parter conceived as a cost-saving exercise, the only serial set entirely within the TARDIS, plays up the friction among the regulars that had dissipated in the course of their adventures in the stone age and on Skaro. Here, a 'faulty spring' and a plunge to the beginning of time are the problem, but the manifestation goes beyond the usual *Star Trek*-style falling about and flying sparks to work on the mood of the crew, who snap at each other as if they were still in the untransmitted pilot and eventually resolve the conflicts that simmered and seethed throughout the first two serials. Thereafter, there would be philosophical disputes – over whether to interfere with established history in 'The Aztecs' (1964), an inter-TARDIS tiff expanded upon when the Doctor runs into the Monk, who wants to help King Harold win the Battle of Hastings – but the regulars would have few real personal differences. The downside of this is that, aside from the Doctor's many quirks, they would also have less depth, reduced to stereotypes like action hero or screamer.

Another mystery element introduced in 'An Unearthly Child' is resolved so swiftly that the title gives it away: the solution to the puzzle of Susan is that she really is from another planet. And, crucially, another time. As in many other details, the first episode differs from the concept *Doctor Who* would settle on: here, the Doctor and Susan, 'wanderers in the fourth dimension', are 'exiles ... cut off from our own planet, without friends or protection'. Though pop fan Susan ♥s the 1960s, the Doctor sniffs 'I tolerate this century, but I don't enjoy it' and muses

19

wistfully 'but one day we shall get back'. This element was swiftly dropped: the First Doctor never again mentions that he's looking for his planet or further explains how he came to be exiled from it. At the end of 'The Massacre' (aka 'The Massacre of St Bartholomew's Eve', 1966), temporarily bereft at the departure of all his companions, he even considers going back but then howls 'but I can't' in an unusual display of raw emotion that still doesn't clarify whether this means he is unable to pilot the TARDIS there or circumstances on his own world mean he wouldn't be welcome. Attempts to go home are not the series' equivalent of the search for the one-armed man who really killed Mrs Kimble on *The Fugitive* (1963–8). Science-fiction shows on the lost in space (or time) theme popped up quickly (*The Time Tunnel*, 1966–7; *Battlestar Galactica*, 1978–9), but the neverending journey to an unreached destination formula of *Wagon Train* (1958–64) and *Rawhide* (1961–6) did not work in this context.

In 'The War Games', the serial which finally named the Time Lords and gave answers to questions the audience had nearly forgotten, the Doctor (now Patrick Troughton) is seen to have fled from an advanced but boring civilisation of do-nothing observers. This was a canny change, understanding as American shows did not that a) viewers who enjoyed the adventures didn't want to listen to whining characters who only wanted to get home and live boring lives (some Kansas residents have voiced objection to the ending of *The Wizard of Oz*, 1939) and b) random wandering can be prolonged for decades whereas protracted quests for home tend to provoke cancellation before the storyline is resolved. Richard Kimble cleared his name but, as far as television viewers are concerned, the Space Family Robinson are still lost. For the bulk of the series' run, the Doctor and his companions were lost too, with a long stretch marooned on Earth for Jon Pertwee and frequent overrides of the TARDIS from the Time Lords – in the post-Watergate era committed to a policy of covert intervention, using the deniable Doctor as an agent – to dump their loose cannon in various trouble spots to clear up messes they were too high minded to sully themselves with.

These days, courtesy of omnibus repeats and video/DVD releases, *Doctor Who* tends to be viewed as if it consisted of a run of feature-length stories, rather than as it was originally intended – a series of serials, with cliffhangers and reprises and catch-up scenes to fill in those who might have missed an episode along the way. Though rarely considered as such, the first serial could be taken as a stand-alone introduction, 'An Unearthly Child', followed by a three-part serial ('100,000 BC'). This means that when the serial is watched in a lump, all manner of interesting and intriguing things are set up in the first episode but set aside in favour of something else. The shadow of an axe-wielding caveman, approaching the TARDIS for the show's first cliffhanger (incidentally, a clever perspective trick), carries over from the set-up into the first proper story, just as 'The Firemaker' ends on Skaro, with the Doctor and companions leaving the TARDIS as the radiation detector swings into the 'danger' zone.[9] In early seasons, *Who* blurred the distinctions between individual serials by closing each story with a teaser for the next, a strategy adopted by *Lost in Space* and a few other American programmes; this would be decommissioned, reduced to the occasional mention of a just-defeated monster or explanation for a costume change, revived only for special occasions, like the summons to Gallifrey at the end of 'The Hand of Fear' (1976) that leads into the precedent-setting revelations of 'The Deadly Assassin' (1976) or the increasingly elaborate prep for the regenerations that close 'Planet of the Spiders' (1974), 'Logopolis' (1981) and 'The Caves of Androzani' (1984).

21

In its early days, *Doctor Who* seasons spanned up to ten months of the year, stressing its feel as a continuous adventure, but also necessitating a variety of tones which is too often seen as a simple division between 'science-fiction' (or 'monster') and 'historical' (or 'costume') serials. Inconsistency was built into the format from the outset, to the eventual frustration of fans who would like to hammer the whole series into some overarching design. Though the TARDIS might phase from one story to another with a few wheezes, each materialisation was also a reset: trips to the past could be tragedy ('The

Aztecs', 'The Massacre'), swashbuckling adventure ('The Reign of Terror', 1964; 'The Smugglers', 1966), sophisticated farce ('The Romans', 1965), genre pastiche ('The Gunfighters', 1966) or studio epic ('Marco Polo', 1964; 'The Crusade', 1965). The regular cast adapt their established characters to suit not only the period but the overall tone of a given run of episodes: Steven (Peter Purves) sees the Paris of Catherine de Medici as a real place and expresses anguish and frustration at his inability to avert the historically ordained massacre of the Huguenots but treats the Tombstone of Wyatt Earp as a theme park and enjoys dressing and talking as if he were a character in a Western movie though that story too winds up with a bloodbath.

After the phasing out of history in favour of monsters, individual stories became more discrete, seasons briefer and similar-in-tone serials clumped together – as in the *Quatermass*-like threat-to-Earth shows of Jon Pertwee's tenure or the runs of horror- or comedy-themed serials that marked Tom Baker's period. This helped when it came to repackaging stories for stand-alone repeats or, later, video and DVD release. Perhaps lost in this change was a sense of currency, though it has to be said that making a science-fiction show with all the genre's attendant effects and design challenges on the same production basis as a soap opera with five hold-over sets was at best brave and at worst foolhardy. The formal stringing together of separate stories into sagas like 'The Key to Time' (Season 16, 1978–9) or 'The Trial of a Time Lord' (Season 23, 1986), the looser 'E-Space' and 'Black Guardian' trilogies (or the 'Bad Wolf' plot thread of 2005) are attempts to revive the continuous feel of the early days and also to maintain a steady audience. The comings and goings of companion characters also impose narrative across serials and seasons (and Doctors). Sarah Jane Smith (Elisabeth Sladen) or Adric (Matthew Waterhouse) have their own arcs, related to but separate from the Doctor's journeys: Sarah Jane even showed up without him, in the *K-9 and Company* singleton 'A Girl's Best Friend' (1981). In practice – cast departures were more often a case of an actor getting fed up and wanting out than of any desire to develop characters – this often boiled down to giving a character a fairly elaborate build-up then kicking them out with the minimum of fuss. Leela (Louise Jameson) has a strong introduction in 'The Face of Evil' (1977), which revolves around her and her world, but is hastily married off to a spear-carrier at the end of 'The Invasion of Time' (1978). A median approach was taken with Jo Grant (Katy Manning): established solidly in 'Terror of the Autons' (1971), she remained a constant, unchanging presence for three seasons, then had a final serial, 'The Green Death' (1973), built almost entirely around her departure.

Having assembled the four regular cast members inside the TARDIS in 'An Unearthly Child', the show's long voyage begins when, against Susan's protests, the Doctor removes the machine from Totter's Lane, apparently throwing it at random into the streams of time (and, later, space). A process which would become calmer is first envisioned as painful and traumatic, and the distorted graphics from the titles are used to indicate that some vast gulf is being travelled. The first trip is back in time; as in the maiden voyage of H. G. Wells' time machine, the TARDIS might not even have moved at all in space, materialising on the spot which will become the junkyard. Since the journey is shown from inside the police box, with the travellers suffering as they are wrenched through the years, elements later ritualised as essentials are withheld. There is no materialisation scene of the TARDIS seeming to fade into existence in an alien landscape, and the distinctive wheezing dematerialisation sound effect, which would often blend into the first notes of Grainer's theme, is saved for the second trip, at the end of Episode Four ('The Firemaker'). Then, the TARDIS travels from the Earth's prehistory to the planet Skaro at a period identified with our future. Generations after a nuclear holocaust, the humanoid races of Skaro have devolved into epicene Thals and mutant Daleks, as Wells' future humanity have divided into Eloi and Morlocks. So, in its first serials, *Doctor Who* probes the beginning and the end of human civilisation.

'The Cave of Skulls' picks up with the last image of 'An Unearthly Child' (recreated approximately, as would be the case for a while, rather than a reprise of the footage seen the previous week) but leaves the Doctor and companions inside the TARDIS for a few minutes to introduce guest cast and characters in a scene that establishes their particular quandary (the leader who knew the secret of 'making fire' has died without passing it on and two prospective successors jostle for position) and the broad-strokes tones of their society (nasty, brutish and superstitious). This strategy would be reused ever after, sometimes giving over a third of an Episode One to establishing scene and situation before the TARDIS materialises. Just once, with 'Mission to the Unknown' (1965), *Doctor Who* would devote an entire episode to this (allowing the overworked regular cast to have a holiday) without even bringing on the Doctor, setting up 'The Daleks' Master Plan' (1965–6), which would start properly after an intervening historical 'The Myth Makers' (1965). Considering that '100,000 BC' was laying down a formula rather than following it, it is unsurprising that some notes are sounded which would rarely be heard again. The cavemen Za (Derek Newark) and Kal (Jeremy Young) are the prototypes of antagonists found in many, if not most, *Doctor Who* serials. Za, son of the previous ruler, is well intentioned, while Kal is brutal and sneaky. After equivocation and without really making a decision, the Doctor intervenes on the side of the goody, though it is Ian (who makes fire boy scout-fashion) who teaches Za that co-operation is better than tyranny ('Kal is not stronger than the whole tribe'), while the still-ambivalent

24

100,000 BC

Doctor's most notable contribution is encouraging the cavemen to expel the murderous Kal by casting the first stone at him.

In future serials, Za and Kal would turn up again, often expanded into whole factions like the Thals and Daleks of 'The Daleks', Menoptra and Zarbi of 'The Web Planet' (1965) or the Scots rebels and English oppressors of 'The Highlanders' (1966–7). Time after time, the Doctor (taking over long-range thinking from Ian) would aid underdogs against tyrants, solve specific problems, unite disparate factions, defeat a particularly formidable enemy and leave society improved on his departure. This more or less happens in '100,000 BC', but the course is less smooth than it would become: the barbarity of the Stone Age reduces even the calm, humane Barbara to hysterics, and the reaction of the tribe to being gifted with fire is not to allow the travellers to depart in peace with the gratitude of all but to imprison them in a cave, intent on absorbing new blood into the gene-pool. Here, Ian tries to change the nature of the cavepeople, while the Doctor cynically exploits it; all the travellers want to do is leave, and their efforts are aimed at that. Later, they would be more considered, more disposed to intervene on the side of right. And the downtrodden would be less embittered, treacherous and dangerous. In its edginess, spasms of despair and sense of danger – it's so early in the run that any of the characters could be killed off – '100,000 BC' has some of the feel of episodes of *The Avengers* made before the cool familiar formula of unflappable and untouchable heroes gelled and John Steed (Patrick MacNee) was a manipulative, callous charmer and Cathy Gale (Honor Blackman) expressed anguish and resentment at the dirty spying business she was caught up in.

In the early years, the balance of history and science fiction made for an inconsistent attitude. In 'The Aztecs', the serial in which Hartnell's Doctor woos a South American matron,[10] conflict comes between the Doctor, who argues *against* interfering, and Barbara, who tries in a nannyish way to convince the Aztecs to abandon the practice of human sacrifice. Just as the Doctor would later clash with the Monk over meddling with Earth's history, he cautions Barbara against setting up ripples in the continuum – here, by strengthening the Aztecs so that they might stand against Cortez. The Monk needs to be defeated by the Doctor, so that Harold still loses the Battle of Hastings, but Barbara is thwarted by a device found in many time-travel stories: her efforts to change the past are resisted by the tides of history and wind up contributing to the injustices she hopes to end. Barbara's campaign against sacrifice only serves to make the practice more entrenched. When the TARDIS departs there's a downbeat tone (for once, the baddies have won) which would be echoed in other historicals where a few individuals might be helped but a defeat for the forces of good remains on the history books: in 'The Massacre', the protestants of Paris still get wiped out in 1572. This factor, as much as the popularity of monster-themed science-fiction serials, might account for the phasing out of purely historical stories from 'The Highlanders' until the brief, atypical-for-other-reasons reprise of 'Black Orchid' (1982) – which still takes care to include a monster.

With deeper thought in the 1970s, it was established that the timeline of Earth needs to be actively protected: when Sarah Jane reasons in 'Pyramids of Mars' (1975) that there's no point getting into more danger since she knows the Earth *wasn't* destroyed by the Martian–Egyptian Sutekh in 1911, the Doctor (Tom Baker) takes a trip forward to her time to show the ravaged ruin it will become if they don't make a stand. An innovation of the revival, in line with a policy of tackling obvious major or minor variations on the format that hadn't been tackled in the original run, is to have a character attempt to intervene in *personal* history. In 'Father's Day' (2005), Rose (Billie Piper) averts her father's death in a car accident in 1987 only to find the forces of the continuum resist the alteration and threaten to fold up the universe and start again. When the TARDIS arrives on another planet or in the future, the limitation of fidelity to history is removed, allowing for triumphs like the defeat of the occupying Daleks in 'The Dalek Invasion of Earth', the rescue of the ugly-but-nice Rills rather than the beautiful-but-nasty Drahvins from a doomed planet in 'Galaxy 4' (1965) or the thwarting of the invasion of peaceful Dulkis by alien imperialists in 'The Dominators' (1968). Mostly forgotten in all this is that the Doctor comes from 'another time' as well as 'another world'. For him, there should be no difference between meddling in the history of Earth and that of Skaro; if it's wrong to save Britain from the Norman Conquest in 1066, why isn't it wrong to save 2064 Earth from the Daleks or Dulkis from the Dominators? This is addressed obliquely once (in 'Genesis of the Daleks') and never resolved, though (over decades) the Time Lords change from refusing to intervene in the lives of lesser beings into feeling an obligation to police the time-streams without being seen to do so.

Individual Time Lords – good like the Doctor, mischievous like the Monk or evil like the Master – almost never carry out the race's stated policies. In 'City of Death' (1979), the alien Scaroth (Julian Glover) plans to tinker with time to allow his race to survive, though it means life on Earth will never evolve. The Doctor cautions him against interfering with history and Scaroth quite justifiably complains 'but it's all you ever do', whereupon Baker's Time Lord dismisses the objection with an airy 'but I'm a professional'. If we're to take this as more than just a snappy comeback –a debatable point in that this is the script that most benefits from Douglas Adams' way with a smart line – then professionalism has come late in the game. Hartnell and Troughton play the Doctor as a well-meaning amateur given to rash actions that often don't turn out well. Even after the erratic, selfish streak of early Hartnell was banished, plots would frequently be furthered by the Doctor being too clever for his own good: in Episode One, Troughton can't resist solving a puzzle that leads to the revival of old enemies in 'The Tomb of the Cybermen' (1967); in 'Bad Wolf' (2005), Eccleston revisits a space station a hundred years after saving the day in 'The Long Game' (2005) only to find that his intervention in an earlier injustice has served to make things catastrophically worse.

Jon Pertwee's Doctor went so far as to have a job (unpaid) as 'scientific advisor' to UNIT and was given to the sort of campaigning one might expect from a radical 1970s boffin: lobbying for a ban on a cruel entertainment form in 'Carnival of Monsters' (1973), allying with an ecologically minded commune in 'The Green Death'. Baker half-heartedly kept this up, though he would drift away from UNIT rather than resign. Like Pertwee, he worked also for the Time Lords, who were prone to overriding his TARDIS and dumping him in galactic trouble spots, which at least suggested an explanation for the fact that every place the Doctor ever visited turned out to be under threat from some sort of evil. Pertwee's Doctor and Baker's Doctor both grumbled about this hypocritical manipulation, then got the job done – but Baker was less biddable. In 'Genesis of the Daleks', the Time Lords want him to alter history so that the Daleks will be destroyed shortly after their creation, but he reasons that some good – a great planetary coalition prompted by the threat – will come from evil, and fudges the job, delaying but not destroying the Daleks. Of course, this serves the ends of the programme rather than the designs of the Time Lords – the Daleks were too popular to be written out of continuity, and this serial made several changes (the introduction of Davros, for instance) that enabled a played-out menace to be reinstated.

It is impossible to overestimate the importance of the Daleks to *Doctor Who*.

If the series had remained faithful to Sydney Newman's 'no monsters' decree, it would have lasted a year or two and now be about as well remembered as *Object Z* (1965), *Counterstrike* (1969) or *The Guardians* (1971). Given that it tries to do *Quest for Fire* (1981) 'as live' in the studio, '100,000 BC' holds up surprisingly well. Its atmosphere of incipient violence (a pile of skulls with axe-holes) established the horrific thread that would remain central to the format and make the show a target for clean-up-television campaigners. However, it's now impossible to watch the serial without considering the series' subsequent development. '100,000 BC' is as notable for things which would not be followed through as for elements endlessly elaborated and reprised. *Doctor Who* might have benefited from keeping up the first serial's comparative realism, in messy human drama as well as archaeology. But, for 1963 audiences, the show *really* started with the cliffhanger of 'The Dead Planet', Episode One of 'The Daleks'. While exploring an apparently deserted all-metal city on Skaro, Barbara is separated from her companions and becomes uncharacteristically panic-stricken as

28

doors open and close automatically and she is lost in the first of the series' many futuristic corridors. Suddenly, she is menaced by the point of view of something with a telescopic, sucker-tipped arm.

The reverse shot, showing us what a Dalek looks like, is withheld for a week, but Barbara's scream suggests a terrifying sight. When the first appearance of the Daleks topped a poll of memorable TV moments, most voters misremembered it – assuming that, as with many subsequent monsters, a Dalek has a full reveal at the fade-out of 'The Dead Planet' and squawks its first threat before the credits roll. Not so. Indeed, when the scene is restaged at the beginning of 'The Survivors', Episode Two, Barbara's full-throated scream becomes a panicky gulp and the proper entrance of *Doctor Who*'s most recurrent villains and most iconic image (more so even than the TARDIS) is delayed further. As in many future cliffhanger reprises, we are taken up to the 'but what happens next?' moment only to cut away to other business, in this case the Doctor exploring elsewhere. The shape of the Daleks is foreshadowed by a security camera eyestalk swivelling on a wall and – echoing the Krel doorway in *Forbidden Planet* (1956) – alien architecture which uses low ceilings, lopsided parabola-arch doorways and smooth floors to suggest squat, non-human beings have built the city. Even before the Daleks glide on-screen, the city has conveyed a sense of their metal aesthetic – which is apt in that writer Terry Nation's creations entered 1960s pop consciousness thanks to Raymond Cusick's remarkable *design*.

29

The Daleks are actually introduced when the Doctor, Ian and Susan enter a room and the camera pulls back with a very Dalek-like movement, to reveal four of the things, menacingly aiming their extensions at the travellers. Besides the eyestalk and the sucker, there's a stubbier device soon identified as a weapon. One of the creatures speaks, issuing orders in a distinctive, halting mechanical croak that would be imitated by every child in the land. 'You will move ahead of us and follow our di-rections. This way – im-mediately!' The Doctor and Susan comply, but Ian hesitates. The Dalek raises its voice pettishly, insisting '*I said im-mediately!*' The problem of indicating which of the identical, mouthless Daleks is speaking is solved by flashing ear-eye-like lights on the upper dome to show which Dalek is issuing commands or making threats. Ian makes a run for it and the Dalek gives an order to itself ('Fire!', not the more familiar 'Ex-ter-min-ate'). In another of the simple, effective inventions that distinguish the first weeks of *Doctor Who*, the weapon's energy discharge is conveyed by briefly flashing a negative image accompanied by a whooshing sound effect. The cinema films opt for plumes of prettily coloured smoke, suggesting some sort of gas weapon, but the television show would only refine the effect by upgrading to colour negative, limiting the reversal to a patch of the picture to indicate the area being exterminated and adding an x-ray flash that illuminates the skeleton of a given victim. Ian is temporarily crippled, rather than ex-ter-min-at-ed, indicating a 'phasers on stun' setting for Dalek weaponry rarely used again.

Barbara asks 'Do you think they really are just machines?' When she suggests there might be 'someone inside them', Susan giggles hysterically (a credible reaction) but Barbara has made the right guess[11]. The Doctor, suffering more than the others from Skaro's ambient radiation, is given the backstory by a chatty, arrogant Dalek. Five hundred years previously, in 'the neutronic war', Skaro's antagonistic humans became separate races. The Dals devolved into mutant creatures not fully seen outside their casings (we will get nasty glimpses of slime, claw and tentacle over the years and a full reveal in 2005) and retreated to their city 'protected by our machines'. Though the etymology would be revised in 'Genesis of the Daleks', when Nation decided the human Dalek precursors were the Kaleds, the initial thought seems to be that a mutant Dal only becomes a Dalek when bonded with its shell, which is a combination of iron lung and armoured vehicle. The few surviving Thals dwell in the petrified outlands, thanks to a drug which counters radiation sickness (the MacGuffin of the next stretch of the story). In a feint soon abandoned, the Dalek history lesson is slanted to suggest that the Thals ('disgustingly mutated') are even more dangerous than the Daleks. The Doctor, ready to overlook imprisonment and extermination, guesses the Thals were the side that dropped the Bomb, which may well be true – they were warriors, while the Dals were 'teachers and philosophers'. We know better: unseen Thals left samples of their drug outside the TARDIS in Episode One. Susan, the only prisoner healthy enough to venture out of the city, is despatched by the Daleks to obtain the drug, which – of course – they intend to use for their own purposes, leaving the humans to die horribly.

By now, we should have pegged the Daleks as fascists.

They exploit the presence of the intruders in order to lure the Thals into peace negotiations which are (of course) a move in a plan to wipe out the other race. The message is that appeasement doesn't work with Daleks. The revelation about the Thals is that they are not ugly mutants, but a tribe of drama school-accented Adonises and Aphrodites (including starlet Virginia Wetherell) in padded tunics and bondage britches (though much less effete than the glitter-made-up blondies of the film *Dr Who and the Daleks*, 1965). By 1963, identification of the hostile alien with the Cold War enemy was almost complete in American media science fiction: film after film presented emotionless hive minds (often from the 'red planet') as a threat to the American way of life. *Invaders from Mars* (1953) presents a perfect caricature of America's idea of a Stalinist society: a big brain in a glass bubble issuing orders to hulking, bug-eyed drones. Whether applying military might (*The War of the Worlds*, 1953) or creeping subversion (*Invasion of the Body Snatchers*, 1956), these aliens were analogous with the threat of Soviet communism. *The Thing from Another World* (1951) first strikes an Arctic base that is NATO's front line of defence against Russian attack, as does a less impressive monster in *The Deadly Mantis* (1957). After Sputnik and the terrifying prospect of enemy superiority in space, the red menace became more cartoonishly evil – zapping a faithful dog to a skeleton in *Teenagers from Outer Space* (1958). British science fiction occasionally ran along these lines (as in *The Trollenberg Terror*, 1958) but a nation that had suffered the Blitz and the direct threat of Nazi invasion still harked back to World War II for its nightmares.

The Daleks are perfect little Hitlers: ordering, obeying, exterminating, ranting in unison, rolling over enemies, consumed with race hatred, merciless, untrustworthy (they never make a treaty they don't break), rotten to the core. Though they seem to be individuals, they act as one – lacking even names, let alone differentiations of personality. In later serials, this would prove a dramatic problem, necessitating the creation of Führer figures like the SS-coloured Black Dalek of 'The Dalek Invasion of Earth' (1964) and the towering but immobile Emperor Dalek of 'The Evil of the Daleks' and 'The Parting of the Ways'. Often, a human villain works in collaboration with the Daleks, memorably the Quisling-like 'Guardian of the Solar System', Mavic Chen (Kevin Stoney), of 'The Daleks' Master Plan' and the ultimately Dalek-minded Victorian inventor, Theodore Maxtible (Marius Goring), in 'The Evil of the Daleks'. While 'The Daleks' is full of parallels with Word War II, the Daleks' first return, in 'The Dalek Invasion of Earth', goes even further: a full-scale occupation with collaborators, black marketeers, looting, a Resistance movement, ruthless reprisals for acts of sabotage, slave workers and concentration camps. Elements, like a ruined London dominated by alien machines, are drawn from Wells' Martian invasion, but Nation keeps sampling occupied France and Blitzed Britain. This scrambling almost shifts the serial into the 'if Britain had fallen' subgenre: much-reproduced stills of Daleks parading in Trafalgar Square or on London Bridge have the same frisson as similarly snatched scenes with Nazi officers strutting against tourist landmarks in *It Happened Here* (1966).

The Daleks were instantly popular with children, triggering the first flood of *Doctor Who* merchandise (much featuring Daleks but *not* the Doctor) and making it a priority for the production team to circumvent the race's destruction at the climax of 'The Daleks' to bring them back again and again. After the imitable ex-ter-min-ate croak, a reason for their great appeal was that Daleks were easy for kids to *draw* – no fiddly hands or facial features, an appealing mix of grilles, roundels (echoing the TARDIS?), domed carapace and add-on implements. Less anthropomorphised than most film and TV robots (strictly speaking, they're cyborgs), the Daleks blend opposite extremes of science-fiction menace: regimented, dystopian, mechanical hard outer shell and seething, tentacled, messy soft inner creature. Many later monsters remain men in rubber suits (cf: Ice Warriors, Silurians, Zygons, Terileptils, Slitheen), but the Daleks aren't even identifiable as human by the way they move. Other mechanical races (cf: Mechanoids, Cybermen, Movellans) are inhumanly emotionless, ruthlessly logical and therefore perfect straight men to a clownish hero as well as a threat to his way of life. By contrast, the Daleks brag about their superior intellect but act like toddlers in perpetual hissy fits. In this, they are the perfect playground monsters, utterly evil but also utterly childish. Just like any gang of murderous bullies, the Daleks gloat when in power ('Advance and attack! Attack and destroy! Destroy and rejoice!') and throw tantrums when thwarted ('Can-not control! Can-not control!'). When

33

Captured by the Daleks!

the Second Doctor tinkers with their essential nature in 'The Evil of the Daleks', he fulfils the fantasies of 60s kids who loved their Dalek toys by creating *benignly* childish creatures. A rare cliffhanger featuring not danger but triumph comes with the revelation that three trundling Daleks are indulging in a hitherto-unexpected activity, playing choo-choo trains.

34   The initial dramatic limitation of the Daleks was that – very *unlike* the Nazis – the race has no internal dissent. This produces one great ironic moment in 'The Power of the Daleks' (1966): a temporary alliance is made between a few Daleks surviving in a universe which has forgotten them and one faction in an Earth colony riven by internecine strife, prompting an uncharacteristically philosophical Dalek, who can't understand a race that *doesn't* agree on everything, to muse 'Why would a hu-man want to kill another hu-man?' From 'The Evil of the Daleks' onward, Dalek plots contrive factions within the race or come up with alien allies (the Ogrons) or enemies (the Movellans) to dilute their sameyness. The Daleks would gain a recognisable figurehead in Davros, introduced in 'Genesis of the Daleks' (1975) and prominent in subsequent Dalek stories until 'Remembrance of the Daleks' (1988).[12] Davros (initially Michael Wisher, later Terry Molloy) is a transitional stage between human (or Kaled/Dal) and Dalek, the founder of the race. A one-armed mutant in a mobile chair that resembles the lower half of a Dalek, with a single mechanical eye in the centre of his forehead, Davros

is given to Hitlerian rants and proves so inept a leader that he seems permanently on the point of being assassinated by his ruthless minions. Eventually, Davros gets caught up in a Dalek civil war whose revised history extends over serials made years apart by production teams hung up on an ever-shifting continuity but excited by the notion of a power struggle between the Black Dalek and the Emperor Dalek decades after casual viewers had forgotten who they were.

As the series' most recurrent villain, suffering enough defeats to be classed as the losers of the universe rather than its conquerors, the Daleks became difficult to take seriously. A certain mockery creeps in as early as 'The Escape', Episode Three of 'The Daleks' – when Ian replaces the mutant inside a Dalek carapace and gets laughs with his distorted voice. In David Whitaker's 'The Power of the Daleks', the first Dalek serial not scripted by Nation, a strain of subtler black humour emerges as Daleks glide around humans pretending to be helpful, adopting a faintly mocking catchphrase ('I am your ser-vant'). The joshing carried beyond the show: the Daleks frequently appear in newspaper cartoons (a 1964 Illingworth singleton in the *Daily Mail* shows NATO politicians menaced by 'the Degaullek'), novelty records (the Go Go's' 'I'm Gonna Spend My Christmas with a Dalek'), comedy programmes (a Spike Milligan sketch about a Pakistani Dalek on one of his Q [1975–80] shows) or TV ads ('peace and love'-chanting *hare krishna* Daleks hawking some product I've forgotten).[13]

A long-standing joke about physical limitations that didn't matter when the Daleks were confined to their metal city (and the studio floor) was finally written into 'Destiny of the Daleks' (1979), typical of the Douglas Adams-overseen self-parody of the late Tom Baker period: the Doctor escapes to an upper level of a complex and sneers at the inability of the self-declared 'master race of the universe' to climb stairs. A fanboy answer, typical of the humourless patching-up of continuity 'flaws' in the latter days of the show, came in 'Remembrance of the Daleks': a cliffhanger is built around the shocking revelation that a Dalek can now levitate up the cellar stairs. This served as a precedent for 'Dalek' (2005), where a lone Dalek levitates implacably up a *lot* of stairs, and 'The Parting of the Ways', in which – adapting an image from 1960s Dalek annuals – regimented armies float in formation through the void to attack a space station. It became difficult to wring scares out of evil aliens so thoroughly absorbed into teatime culture that they were in danger of becoming cosy (there were Dalek *soft* toys). Some Dalek serials – 'Genesis of the Daleks' and 'Resurrection of the Daleks' (1984) in particular – go overboard to re-establish their menace by delivering some of the grimmest, most violent, most depressing, high body-count episodes in *Who* history. 'Dalek', a reintroduction even more crucial than that of the Doctor (Christopher Eccleston) in 'Rose', is a concerted attempt to make the monster scary again, even as it reprises 'The Evil of the Daleks' by having its lone Dalek – which an unwary collector wants to call a 'metaltron' – absorb 'the human factor' from the kindly touch of Rose, who has no idea what the thing is and instinctively feels for its plight as a torture victim. Here, the Doctor is prompted to a rare display of panic and homicidal fury by the first croak and flash of the Dalek's lights in a darkened cell, and a new backstory is filled in whereby the Time Lords have succeeded (provisionally) in wiping the Daleks out of history – their aim as far back as 'Genesis of the Daleks' – but have become all but extinct themselves in the process.

'The Daleks' (1963–4) established *Doctor Who* as a hit show. It also ran over budget across the stretch of seven episodes,

Vicky (Maureen O'Brien) and the Doctor

necessitating a single-set 'bottle show' two-parter 'The Edge of Destruction' to carry the series over into the full-costume 'historical' 'Marco Polo'. The stopgap measure provided essential character development and resolution: after the effects of a TARDIS malfunction wear off, the four regulars have worked through ingrained problems with each other and future disagreements will be less personal, based on misunderstanding or philosophical disagreements. Without this catharsis, the interactions of the four characters would have been less predictable but also so volatile that it might have been difficult to keep the series going. There's a sense that 'Marco Polo' is what the BBC *really* wanted: whereas '100,000 BC' is a fantasy of prehistory about made-up characters, 'Marco Polo' has the TARDIS materialise in known history, and has the Doctor meet people (led by Mark Eden as the Italian explorer) who can be looked up in school textbooks. A problem, of course, is that the regular characters can't really *do* anything – in 'Assassin at Peking', the final episode, it is Marco Polo who has the sword-fight with the murderous Mongol Tegana (Derren Nesbitt) to save the life of Kublai Khan (Martin Miller). The Doctor and companions advise the hero that Tegana is a rotter, but otherwise stand back and let things happen. Writer John Lucarotti, obviously aware of this shortcoming, constructed his next script ('The Aztecs') around what might happen if Barbara wasn't content to let history take its course.

37

The remainder of the first season delivered more serials on the pattern of 'The Daleks' ('The Keys of Marinus', 'The Sensorites') and 'Marco Polo' ('The Aztecs', 'The Reign of Terror'). Only 'The Aztecs' does much to stretch the regulars beyond siding with the oppressed, escaping captivity, helping out in various tasks (collecting the plot coupons of Marinus), doing their established shtick (Hartnell blustery, Russell steadfast, Hill thoughtful, Ford panicky) and running from peril to peril. Audience figures, boosted during 'The Daleks', gradually fell off, only to rise again in the second season with 'The Dalek Invasion of Earth' and hold steady. Terry Nation's second Dalek story was the serial which ensured the show's longevity, not only by gaining high ratings but also by demonstrating a willingness to repeat and develop concepts that had elicited a strong audience response and accepting the necessity of change even within the out-of-time construct of the TARDIS.

2 Regeneration

Most accounts of the change-over between the First Doctor and the Second concentrate on production circumstances:[14] William Hartnell's increasing infirmity (leading to line fluffs preserved for ever for broadcast) and peppery demand for more script control (hotly resisted by the production team), the casting of Patrick Troughton and the development of his take on the character, even the question of whether *Doctor Who* could continue without its established star.

However, all this went on behind the scenes. As far as the audience is concerned, what happened was this ... On 29 October 1966, at the end of Part Four of 'The Tenth Planet', the Doctor and his current companions – seaman Ben Jackson (Michael Craze) and dolly bird Polly (Anneke Wills) – returned to the TARDIS after defeating the Cybermen, who had debuted in this serial. The Doctor, more exhausted by this battle than all his previous adventures ('this old body ... is wearing thin'), had a funny turn and collapsed. In a shimmering close-up, his face seemed to change into that of a younger, darker man. Actually, the close-up was so close and the average TV set so small it was quite hard to read the difference between the Doctor's faces and viewers might not even have noticed the change. Next week, on Guy Fawkes' Night, at the beginning of Part One of 'The Power of the Daleks', the Doctor jumped up again and was not only over his dizzy spell but transformed into another person entirely. For an episode or two, Ben and Polly weren't even sure this *was* the Doctor – though he had full access to the earlier incarnation's memories, his manner was completely different. Hartnell had been stern, testy, commanding, frustrated when stumbling over his lines, a bit of a bully; Troughton was puckish, quixotic, slyly self-deprecating, using sham fear and panic as a ruse to trick enemies, childishly inquisitive, a 'cosmic hobo'. As the character had evolved in early seasons, Hartnell showed over and over a commitment to fighting tyranny, but often acted like a tyrant himself; Troughton took the Doctor's anti-authoritarian streak as his basic note, and was less demanding of his companions (friends, rather than relations), more given to tootling on his recorder or generally amusing himself. This Doctor only convinced Ben and Polly – and perhaps the audience – that he was who he said he was by again pulling off Hartnell's most famous trick, defeating the Daleks.

There had been minor coverage of the regeneration in grown-up newspapers, but in the 1960s, fictional events were not obsessively covered by the national press. Now, no popular television drama can surprise audiences by writing out a character through murder, marriage or act of God (or have them outed as gay or a serial killer) without a leak making the front pages of the tabloids. In 1966, Harold Wilson got more editorial coverage than Harold Steptoe, coronations were more newsworthy than *Coronation Street*. I remember noticing that the name of the actor credited as 'Dr Who' in the *Radio Times* was different, but not thinking much of it – a mistake, perhaps. If kids were excited about this particular serial, it wasn't because there was a new Doctor but because – after apparently being wiped out in 'Destruction of Time', Episode Twelve of the epic 'The Daleks' Master Plan' (1965–6) – the Daleks were back! A BBC1 trailer included as an extra on the 2004 *Lost in Time* DVD avoids mentioning the change of Doctor while boosting the discovery of a couple of cobwebby, deactivated Daleks. Like the use of the Daleks, this lack of ballyhoo may well have been an insurance policy to keep audiences watching long enough to get used to the idea of a new Doctor.

When the Daleks made their first return in 'The Dalek Invasion of Earth' (1964), the show signalled that it was not following the perceived BBC policy of giving child viewers what was good for them (serials about the Crusades) rather than what they wanted (bug-eyed monsters). Indeed, the Daleks had been such a hit that the production team made concerted efforts to come up with 'the new Daleks',[15] which finally paid off with Kit Pedler and Gerry Davis's Cybermen, cyborg villains more manoeuvrable in the studio and on location than Daleks. These high-pitched, constantly evolving silver troublemakers would become the Second Doctor's most recurrent foes, take a long rest during the tenure of the Third Doctor and show up for token engagements with most subsequent Time Lords. One effect of the popularity of the Daleks, which Hartnell must have noticed, is that *Doctor Who* was less likely to be seen as a star vehicle. The Dalek comic strip in *TV Century 21* (which invented the distinctive typeface used to convey their rasping speech) and a clutch of *Dalek Annuals* did well enough without the Doctor (who had his own Dalek-free strip in the rival *TV Comic*), and the creatures got equal or top billing in the film spin-offs, *Dr Who and the Daleks* (1965) and *Daleks' Invasion Earth 2150 AD* (1966). It was plain that there could be Daleks without *Doctor Who*, as in David Whitaker and Terry Nation's stage play *The Curse of the Daleks* (1965). Peter Cushing's lazy, daffy 'Dr Who' in the films at least tentatively suggested there could be *Doctor Who* without William Hartnell.

41

Of course, all long-running series have to cope with cast changes. *Doctor Who* first tackled this thorny problem in 'Flashpoint', Episode Six of 'The Dalek Invasion of Earth', as Susan (Carole Ann Ford) opts not to travel on in the TARDIS but remain on twenty-first century Earth to help rebuild human civilisation and marry a freedom fighter. As would often be the case, this arises not from logical character development but a performer's decision to quit. In that story, Hartnell, as the Doctor, ad-libs to Ford, as Susan, 'what you need is a jolly good smacked bottom!' This suggests why the twenty-four-year-old actress might have had problems with the way her notionally sixteen-year-old character was being treated by the show. The problem was that it had been established that the Doctor's primary (indeed *only*) personal tie was with his granddaughter. It was reasonably likely that the chick would want to leave the nest, but this left the series stuck for a reason as

Doctor Who (Jon Pertwee)

Doctor Who (Tom Baker)

Doctor Who (Peter Davison)

Doctor Who (Colin Baker)

Doctor Who (Sylvester McCoy)

43

Doctor Who (Paul McGann)

to why the Doctor might continue to haul his departed relative's not-always-congenial teachers about time and space with him. If marrying off Susan was conventional and awkward soap plotting, the strategies devised to replace her and keep Ian and Barbara at least temporarily in the frame were ingenious enough to count as a survival trait. In 'The Rescue' (1965), the TARDIS takes on Vicki (Maureen O'Brien), a spacewrecked and (crucially) orphaned girl, who may be from Earth and the future but serves as a surrogate child for the Doctor and even a new pupil for the other adults.

The inference is that *all* the temporary travelling companions who come and go throughout the series are substitutes for the lost Susan. The 'orphan' gambit whereby a new regular loses an actual or substitute parent during their first adventure would be reprised many times, for example with Victoria (Deborah Watling) in 'The Evil of the Daleks' (1967), whose father (John Bailey) charges the Doctor with looking after her as he is exterminated by the Daleks, and Tegan (Janet Fielding) in 'Logopolis' (1981), whose Aunt Vanessa (Dolores Whiteman) is shrunk to death by the Master (Anthony Ainley). Heroic teamings often arise from such circumstances: the adult orphan Bruce Wayne adopts the bereaved Dick Grayson after the lad's circus aerialist parents have been killed by gangsters in *Detective Comics* No. 38 (1940), which also means Batman takes on Robin as a partner in crime-fighting; a striking deductive exercise in *The Sign of the Four* (1890), involving a much-pawned family watch, reveals that Dr Watson lost a brother to alcoholism and madness (just as Arthur Conan Doyle lost a father) shortly before forming his near-fraternal bond with Sherlock Holmes. The arc of Rose Tyler in *Doctor Who* (2005–) addresses the question of what happens if the Doctor takes a companion who has a mother (Camille Coduri) and boyfriend (Noel Clarke) back home who don't respond well to what seems like her virtual abduction. Even she has a dead father (Shaun Dingwall) in the background to emphasise the Doctor's parental status; Rose's mum even briefly considers the Doctor as a possible replacement husband before settling into exasperated resentment. The notion of surrogate Susans makes retrospective sense of comings and goings which have more to do with production circumstances than the unfolding over decades of any coherent story. As with many of the programme's regenerative traits, the creative team – notably writers, producers and script editors – have been required to make sense of elements beyond their control. Now, the Doctor's tendency to lose relations and companions is a given, not as often evoked as, say, the destruction of Krypton, but still a melancholy element of the hero's make-up. A tiny, easy-to-miss, affecting moment in the Blitz-set 'The Empty Child' (2005) has an elderly man (Richard Wilson) lament that he started World War II 'as a father and grandfather but now am neither' and the Doctor responding 'I know the feeling'.

With Susan/Ford gone, the precedent was set. Ian (William Russell) and Barbara (Jacqueline Hill) returned to contemporary Earth at the end of 'The Planet of Decision', Part Six of 'The Chase' (1965), presumably to pick up their lives and jobs where they had left off. To replace them, the show took on Steven Taylor (Peter Purves), another space-stranded human (an astronaut imprisoned on Mechanus) who made a suitable partner for Vicki. This streamlined trio served as template for several lasting teams: the Doctor handled the thinking, Steven (more obviously a two-fisted adventurer than Ian) the action ('the butch stuff', as Purves put it on a DVD audio commentary) and Vicki the feeling (often stereotypically screaming at the sight of monsters). This mix was recreated for several successful stretches. Witness: the Second Doctor, Jamie (Frazer Hines) and Victoria or Zoe (Wendy Padbury); the Third Doctor (Jon Pertwee), all of UNIT and Jo Grant (Katy Manning); the Fourth Doctor (Tom Baker), Harry Sullivan (Ian Marter) and Sarah Jane Smith (Elisabeth Sladen); and the Ninth Doctor (Christopher Eccleston), Rose (Billie Piper) and omnisexual action man Jack Harkness (John Barrowman). Some characters were perceived as less successful for violating this format: Liz Shaw (Caroline John) was so brainy that she already knew things the Doctor needed to explain to the audience (to add to the confusion, she also had a doctorate), and was

45

replaced by the intrepid but dimmer Jo and then the professionally inquisitive Sarah Jane (a reporter).

Vicki left uniquely by becoming a historical (or at least mythical) character, Cressida, in 'The Myth Makers' (1965), which for once let a time traveller become genuinely involved in a predetermined story.[16] After her departure came a revolving-door period of innovation and failed experiment. Katarina (Adrienne Hill), introduced in 'The Myth Makers' and killed in the next story, 'The Daleks' Master Plan', was a character who *needed* to happen, to remind viewers how strange the now-established *Who* universe really was. Katarina, one of Cassandra's handmaidens, is pulled from her familiar world (which is fairly wretched – after ten years of siege warfare and the destruction of her city) and cracks up when tossed into a hostile far future which she takes to be the realm of unimaginable gods. She dies in circumstances taken as suicidal self-sacrifice, which might also be down to an ancient Trojan's inability to understand what a spaceship is, let alone an air-lock. Killing off (rather than merely writing out) a regular is a crucial step for any series – often a sobering reminder that an adventurous life is dangerous as well as fun, but also serving (like Janet Leigh's death in *Psycho*, 1960) as advance notice that *anything* can still happen. Katarina's departure was hastily scripted by Terry Nation when the production team decided she was unsustainable as a continuing character, but her death still served to underline the seriousness of this particular epic-length serial (first of several attempts at an 'ultimate' *Doctor Who*).

Dodo (Jackie Lane), ineptly dragged on at the end of the last episode of 'The Massacre' (1966) and equally ineptly sidelined in the middle of 'The War Machines' (1966), was judged insufficiently distinguishable from her predecessors – though Polly, her immediate replacement, seemed to be the same girl with a different hairstyle. The Doctor took Dodo on solely because she reminded him of 'my little Susan'. Despite the sorry example of Katarina, the Second Doctor favoured companions from Earth's past. The adventurous Scot Jamie was bewildered enough early on – in 'The Moonbase' (1967), he takes a Cyberman for 'the Phantom Piper of the McCrimmons' – then took the future, alien races and bizarre planets in his stride. Writers only occasionally remembered to play up his 1746 ignorance of modern contraptions: in 'The Wheel in Space' (1968), he has no trouble coping with a space-walk but is astonished by a tape recorder. The primmer Victoria, a miss from 1866, did not adjust as well (though she did wear shorter and shorter skirts). In 'Fury from the Deep', she hopped off the merry-go-round for a then-near future England and another set of surrogate parents because 'every time we go anywhere something awful happens' – something viewers had noticed, prompting a few to muse that the TARDIS must have a 'trouble magnet' circuit which drew it to places and times under threat. Victoria was replaced by Zoe, a 'brainchild' from the future who lost her faith in pure logic and stowed away in the police box to broaden her horizons, taking the Doctor as a tutor; later, Adric (Matthew Waterhouse) was the same character (down to the mathematical aptitude) as a sulky teenage boy rather than a perky teenage girl.

As younger performers took the lead, and the Time Lord's background filled in, the Doctor became more than capable of doing his own fight scenes (Pertwee set a precedent with 'Venusian karate') and expressing genuine human feeling. This raises the never-quite-tackled possibility of romantic, perhaps unethical liaisons between the Doctor and his attractive female companions.[17] A frequent get-out to avoid this was to have adult women dress and act like teenagers or even toddlers,

47

Zoe (Wendy Padbury) as action heroine, 'The Mind Robber'

Sarah Jane (Elisabeth
Sladen) and her second-
favourite Doctor (Tom
Baker)

Romana (Mary Tamm) looks
at the Princess (Lalla
Ward) whose body she will
usurp in the next season,
'The Armageddon Factor'

48

Too many companions to
fit into the TARDIS? Adric
(Matthew Waterhouse),
Tegan (Janet Fielding),
Nyssa (Sarah Sutton)

stressing their substitute child/grandchild status. In 'The Hand of Fear' (1976), the serial which builds to Sarah Jane's departure from the series, Elisabeth Sladen is fashionably outfitted in a set of pink overalls aptly described as making her look 'like Andy Pandy'.[18] A less obvious way out of this thorny patch was to use mature, female guest characters in whom the Doctor could take an almost-unnoticed interest, thus stressing his parent–teacher relationship to the tagalong girls. The Doctor makes up to Cameca (Margot van der Burgh) in 'The Aztecs', hoping to learn how to get into the tomb where the TARDIS is trapped – though Hartnell plays the scenes as if the Doctor is genuinely interested in the lively woman.[19] More typical of this approach is the subtly played spark struck between the Doctor (Troughton) and the grown-up, obviously interesting Dr Corwyn (Anne Ridler) in 'The Wheel in Space' as he asks her first name ('Gemma'), then repeats it approvingly. The Doctor is between daughter surrogates in this story, thus unusually open to emotion; Gemma is killed by the Cybermen in Episode Five, which probably teaches him another lesson about caring too much for individuals rather than trying to save planets. By 'The End of the World' (2005), the Doctor (Eccleston) is hitting on a super-evolved tree woman (Yasmin Bannerman) – she gets killed, too.

49

After the departure of Sarah Jane, Tom Baker handled 'The Deadly Assassin' (1976) uniquely without a sidekick, then acquired Leela (Louise Jameson) in 'The Face of Evil' (1977) and K9 in 'The Invisible Enemy' (1977). These companions scrambled the formulae for supporting regulars, a warrior girl who could do action scenes and a domesticated Dalek arguably cleverer and demonstrably more knowledgeable than the Time Lord. These gimmicks suggest a move towards giving the Doctor partners who aren't as pale beside him as the average short-lived, non-regenerating Earthling. Towards the end of his run, Tom Baker was teamed with a 'Time Lady', Romana (Mary Tamm) who even regenerated (into Lalla Ward). Susan came and went before the Time Lords were invented, and can only be considered retroactively (in 'The Five Doctors', 1983) as one. Romana was created after several serials had visited Gallifrey and explored its conservative society: her character arc was a moderation of a know-it-all head prefect attitude as she learned that the disreputable Doctor was better suited than her fussier elders to practical problem-solving. In 'Warriors Gate' (1981), she too rebels, opting not to return to her home planet and become one of several ex-companions scattered around time and space doing good works among formerly oppressed peoples: Susan on Earth after the Dalek Invasion, Steven on the planet of 'The Savages' (1966), Nyssa (Sarah Sutton) among the leper-like Lazars of 'Terminus' (1983).

Leela and Romana, and even clunky K9, had dramatic possibilities beyond those of Earth-originating companions: Leela, from a tribal backwater planet, allowed for a more successful reprise of Katarina's situation as she had difficulty fitting into worlds that were beyond her imagination (she also needed to be cured of her tendency to kill people), while Romana allowed the show to present yet another Time Lord renegade, uniquely showing how she progresses from embodying the dictates of her society to rejecting them. However, in Baker's final appearances and through the Peter Davison and Colin Baker tenures, *Who* returned to its roots by filling out the TARDIS with screamers, question-askers, miniskirt-and-cleavage pin-ups and clever-but-wrong guess-makers. Davison and Colin Baker seem sometimes like exhausted teachers in a kindergarten-set Dennis Potter play where the roles of babbling kids are taken by adult actors. There are moments, like the 'class outing' of 'Black Orchid' (1982), where the writing and playing are light enough to make the squabbling sidekicks tolerable presences, but more often they come across as smug, squeaking idiots. When Adric became the first regular since poor Katarina to die, blowing himself up (and rendering extinct the dinosaurs) to save history from the Cybermen at the climax of 'Earthshock' (1982), the shattering effect – extending to the soap device of running the end titles without music – was mitigated by the fact that no one, including his friends in the TARDIS, had ever liked him much. After an unhappy season with Bonnie Langford,[20] the slightly more mature Seventh Doctor (Sylvester McCoy) was partnered with a thumping-feeling teenage girl Ace (Sophie Aldred), estranged from her parents rather than an orphan but otherwise an all-purpose mix of Steven/Jamie/UNIT/ Leela action-taker and Vicki/Zoe/Jo/Sarah Jane surrogate Susan. There is a poignant charge to the opening and closing of *Doctor Who* (1996), in which first McCoy and then Paul McGann are found alone in the now-cavernous TARDIS – having learned perhaps that only double heartbreak comes from getting attached to human beings who inevitably up and leave just as a Time Lord is settling into a relationship.

It is one thing to pack off and bring on sidekicks, but another to recast a series' lead. In 1965, Douglas Wilmer completed a successful run as *Sherlock Holmes* for BBC-TV but declined to return; in 1967, Peter Cushing starred opposite Wilmer's Watson (Nigel Stock) in a continuance of the series – but Wilmer had not *created* the role of Sherlock Holmes, and indeed Cushing had played it before (in *The Hound of the Baskervilles*, 1959). Dick York was replaced by Dick Sargent as Samantha's stooge-like husband Darrin halfway through the run of *Bewitched* (1968–72) and jokes about the bald-faced substitution have lingered longer than anything else about the show. Team-effort premises like *Z-Cars*, *Star Trek* and *Mission: Impossible* (1966–73) could bring in new leads – Christopher Pike (Jeffrey Hunter) was Captain of the *Enterprise* in the pilot before James T. Kirk (William Shatner) was appointed and Dan Briggs (Steven Hill) headed up the IMF before Jim Phelps (Peter Graves) got the job – and shuffle the format every season, though there would always be bleats along the lines that Sergeant Bilko was not as funny at Camp Fremont as he had been at Fort Baxter. Though three different guest stars (George Sanders, Otto Preminger, Eli Wallach) played Mr Freeze on *Batman*, the show was so uncommitted to credibility no one much cared – Catwoman even changed race, from Julie Newmar to Eartha Kitt. Sometimes, identification of star with role is so complete an alternative is unthinkable: no one but Peter Falk could play Columbo (though he did not originate the part) and 1960s British TV viewers would not have accepted anyone but Rupert Davies as Maigret (though generations later Richard Harris and Michael Gambon had a go at the role). *Doctor Who* without William Hartnell might have proved as iffy as *Alias Smith and*

51

The Doctor scrambles Jamie's Face, 'The Mind Robber'

Jones (1971–3) without Pete Duel (who died and was replaced by Roger Smith), *The X-Files* (1993–2002) without David Duchovny (who quit and was replaced by Robert Patrick, then came back for the last episode) or *Murder One* (1995–7) without Daniel Benzali (who was replaced by less-bald Anthony LaPaglia in a failed attempt to make the show more appealing).

A year before the Doctor's first regeneration, another British show gambled on an equally risky recasting, as John Steed (Patrick MacNee) ended his partnership with Cathy Gale (Honor Blackman) on *The Avengers* and took on Emma Peel (Diana Rigg). *The Avengers* was another show with an evolving format: Cathy hadn't been Steed's first co-lead (she replaced Ian Hendry's David Keel) and didn't even appear in every episode, though Venus Smith (Julie Stevens) is rarely accorded the full Avenger status she deserves. However, the MacNee–Blackman team turned just another thriller–spy–detective programme into a national institution, and the fact that Diana Rigg was not only accepted but took the show to its greatest popularity proved that not all recastings were disastrous. The limiting factor for most series was that their characters were human beings, and therefore couldn't alter their appearance – though the only reason *Bewitched* didn't use some magical mix-up explanation for Darrin's changing face was lack of imagination. *Doctor Who* was rarely guilty of such a failing: during the shooting of 'The Mind Robber' (1968), Frazer Hines had to take a week off with chicken pox, so a scene was written whereby Jamie is turned into a giant jigsaw and the Doctor uses the wrong face-pieces before he becomes human again, allowing Hamish Wilson to play the role (very well) for an episode or so before the proper state of affairs is restored. Something similar had been proposed as a way of effecting a change of Doctors: in 'The Celestial Toymaker' (1966), Hartnell is turned invisible for a spell – one of several devices employed to allow a regular cast-member to take a holiday – and it was proposed that another actor could be in the role when the Doctor became visible again. The idea didn't take. Among many variations attempted over the years, *Who* never had the Doctor regenerate from one lead to another in the *middle* of a serial – though the Comic Relief spoof 'The Curse of Fatal Death' (1999) ran through most of the Time Lord's then-remaining lives to cast a succession of guest stars.[21]

As a medium, television was evolving in the 1960s, and many shows took the opportunity to upgrade or rethink between seasons. 'Lobster Quadrille' (1964), the final Cathy Gale/Honor Blackman episode of *The Avengers*, is studio-bound, 'as-live' three-camera drama with a few luxurious filmed inserts; 'The Town of No Return' (1965), the first Emma Peel/Diana Rigg show, is on film, with dynamic editing and much location filming; with 'From Venus with Love' (1967), debut episode of Rigg's second (and final) season, *The Avengers* was in colour for export purposes (the UK wouldn't convert to all-channel colour broadcasting until 1970). The BBC were reluctant to take such drastic steps, deeming overseas sales a pleasant side-effect but hardly worth chasing (though a scene-change fade halfway through an average *Doctor Who* episode was encouraged so purchasing broadcasters could run commercials) and for the moment colour was best appreciated by the more cultured BBC2 audience. This means *Doctor Who* mostly looked and felt like the same show with Patrick Troughton in the lead as it had under William Hartnell; changes or developments were already in progress.

A willingness to venture out on location, inherited from still-impressive sequences in *Quatermass II* (1955), was displayed as early as 'The Dalek Invasion of Earth'. The use of a contemporary British

setting for the Hartnell-starring 'The War Machines', easier to realise
than the wilds of Skaro, was picked up by Troughton serials like 'The
Faceless Ones' (1967) and 'Fury from the Deep'. These established a
Doctor Who subgenre of Earthbound, Quatermass-like science fiction,
with London repeatedly invaded and the troops out on the streets to
deal with each new menace – hardly a reassuring sight, especially for
viewers in Northern Ireland. 'The Web of Fear' (1968) and 'The
Invasion' (1968) – which introduce Major (later Brigadier) Lethbridge-
Stewart (Nicholas Courtney) and UNIT – serve as pilots for the
genuinely reworked Who that debuted with 'Spearhead from Space' (in
colour, and – just this once – entirely on film) in 1970. Found locations
could be passed off as the future or outer space, with the then-new
South Bank complex representing the London of 2540 in 'Frontier in
Space' (1973). So many quarries and gravel pits stand in for other
planets (Dulkis in 'The Dominators'; Uxarieus in 'Colony in Space',
1971; Solos, 'The Mutants', 1972; Spiridon, 'Planet of the Daleks',
1973; Exxilon, 'Death to the Daleks', 1974) that it's a joke in 'The
Hand of Fear' when the TARDIS materialises in an actual Earth
quarry. Who never entirely forsook its studio origins: creating the
fantastical worlds of 'The Web Planet' (1965), 'The Mind Robber',
'The Curse of Peladon' (1972) or 'Kinda' (1982) indoors, and playing
up the claustrophobia with single, enclosed locations like the space
station of 'The Ark in Space' (1975), the giant mining machine in 'The
Robots of Death' (1977) or the Edwardian lighthouse of 'Horror of
Fang Rock' (1977). Just as early historicals tried to do the Crusades in
the studio, there were efforts to pull off space opera under the same
circumstances, relying on modelwork far less impressive than that
found in Gerry Anderson's Supermarionation shows for 'The
Moonbase' or 'The Space Pirates' (1969).

With a new Doctor, the show did change emphasis. Stories set
in the past had already shifted tack from broadly educational serials
about people and situations you could find on the O-level syllabus ('The
Massacre') to pure swashbuckling matinée entertainment ('The
Smugglers', 1966). After 'The Highlanders' (1966–7), Troughton's sole

monster-free historical trip, even these were dropped from the mix. The bulk of the Second Doctor's tenure was devoted to monsters, with the variety once provided by periwigs and swordplay provided by an occasional science-fiction adventure. 'The Underwater Menace' (1967), 'The Enemy of the World' (1967–8) and 'The Space Pirates' all offer melodrama rather than monsters (the fish people of 'Underwater' are not the menace) and plots about tyrants or pirates that could once have been played as historical adventures. Just as Hartnell had one outstanding excursion into more playful, if still barbed, fantasy in 'The Celestial Toymaker', Troughton took a trip outside the series' format in 'The Mind Robber'. After a remarkable Episode One (actually, a hastily scripted no-budget fill-in) set in white emptiness with only the TARDIS and some robots, this explores 'the Land of Fiction', where Gulliver and Rapunzel co-exist and all the stories in the universe originate. Often, *Who* tried to transcend the studio, but with 'The Celestial Toymaker' and 'The Mind Robber', the show roots about inside the great prop store and dressing-up trunk of the BBC. What is especially satisfying about these serials is that they delve into the audience's delight in the Doctor's adventures as the Doctor engages in game-play that could be extended infinitely, for the Toyroom and the Land of Fiction are potential homes for a wanderer not yet identified as a Time Lord. Both stories end with escapes into the larger universe of the show, which we recognise as essentially the same enticing–sinister environment the Doctor has supposedly broken free from. After all, *our* Doctor doesn't come from Gallifrey but the Land of Fiction, and his home is as much Toyroom as TARDIS.

55

Troughton was much better at genuine or sham terror than Hartnell and *Doctor Who* became more disposed to all-out horror. Hartnell serials which feature aliens and humans mingling and clashing in outer space are serious about science fiction, and hold back on judgments. 'The Sensorites' (1964), the ugly-but-eventually-decent Rills ('Galaxy 4', 1965) or the servile-but-eventually-oppressive Monoids ('The Ark', 1966) are not depicted as proper monsters. In 'The Web Planet', Hartnell's Doctor even intervenes in a conflict between *two* non-human species, the ant-like Zarbi and the butterfly-like Menoptra – either or both of these races could be considered monsters, and neither is the real villain (it's the disembodied Animus). 'The Macra Terror' (1967), a comparable Troughton serial, establishes a science-fiction situation to explore satiric, moral points – in this case, a colony where apparent contentment is maintained only through behind-the-scenes horrors – but it also has real monsters in the giant crab villains who reach claws into frame to pinch screaming humans. The title alone indicates the tone and subsequent *Who* serial titles frequently include slightly meaningless scary movie buzz-words, 'Terror of . . .', 'Horror of . . .', 'Curse of . . .', '. . . of Death', '. . . of Doom' or '. . . of Blood'. *Who* was tagged early for nightmare aspects but only with the Second Doctor did it begin truly to *earn* its reputation as a frightening programme. Much from this period lodges in the collective memory: the Cybermen returning to life and shredding their plastic shrouds in 'The Tomb of the Cybermen' (1967); the fey, seaweed-possessed zombies (Mr Oak and Mr Quill) of 'Fury from the Deep' breathing out asphyxiating gas from mouths that gape in a silent screech.

  Doctor Who also began to make a concerted effort to recycle, in that any initially popular monster tended to get called back, a privilege previously reserved for the Daleks. 'The Moonbase', the second Cyberman serial, was a virtual remake of the first, 'The Tenth Planet', but 'The Seeds of Death' (1969), the second Ice Warriors serial, could have been lightly rewritten as a vehicle for any other run-of-the-mill invader. This pattern would linger in the show's format, accounting for such same-again efforts as 'Terror of the Autons' (1971), 'Arc of Infinity' (1983), 'Snakedance' (1983) and 'Time and the Rani' (1987). A rare sequel to build upon an effective original was 'The Web of Fear', a follow-up to 'The Abominable Snowmen' (1967). In the manner of 'The Dalek Invasion of Earth', this brings its monsters closer to home, relocating the Yeti from the remote Himalayas in the 1930s to an abandoned London of the near-future. The second take streamlines the slightly cuddly monsters of the first serial into more dangerous-looking creatures, uniquely recalls a youngish character from the first serial

(Jack Watling's Professor Travers) as an old man (surely, time travellers would often bump into people at different times of their lives?) and delivers one of *Who*'s most primal settings, the Yeti-occupied London Underground.

As the Doctor racked up more exploits, elements of continuity were laid down. While the first serials formally ran into one another with epilogue-trailer-cliffhanger episode endings, they were otherwise stand-alone: with each serial, the TARDIS materialised in an entirely fresh situation remote in time and space from previous adventures. The sense of a coherent *Doctor Who* universe, unthinkable at the outset, began with the return of the Daleks in 'The Dalek Invasion of Earth'. A precedent-setting throwaway came in 'The Space Museum' (1965) where a Dalek is found on display in the eponymous tourist attraction, first of many instances of the show referring to its own past – later developed in the clips montages used to recap monsters ('The War Games', 1969), Doctors ('The Brain of Morbius', 1976), companions ('Resurrection of the Daleks', 1984) or the whole story so far ('Mawdryn Undead', 1983). 'The Chase', the third Dalek serial, changes the game slightly: rather than have the TARDIS happen to show up where there was adventure to be had, Terry Nation has his villains initiate the plot by pursuing the TARDIS in their own time machine, intending to exterminate the hero who has defeated them twice. There is a sense, from offhand remarks in 'The Celestial Toymaker' and 'The Savages' that the Doctor (and his companions) are becoming well-known within their wide fictional universe just as the show was becoming famous in reality. 'The Ark', another concept that had to be used once, divides its four episodes into two two-part segments set in the same locale but 700 years apart, with the TARDIS crew helping out one set of characters and then being near-legendary historical figures to their descendants.

Bits of the universe filled in during the 1960s, with the ongoing Dalek saga joined by a parallel Cyberman history and other evil races (the Ice Warriors, the Yeti) managing second bouts with the Doctor. It is impossible to reconcile the futures of Earth presented in every other

57

1960s serial: the ice age of 'The Ice Warriors' (1967) is an unlikely prelude to the temperate, apparently near-future scenario of its own sequel 'The Seeds of Death'; and the twenty-first century seems to exist in alternative versions that include the occupied ruin of 'The Dalek Invasion of Earth', the dictatorship of 'The Enemy of the World' and the spacefaring civilisation of 'The Wheel in Space'. When Lethbridge-Stewart and UNIT showed up in a Cyberman sequel ('The Invasion') after having made a debut in a Yeti sequel ('The Web of Fear'), a first attempt was made to tie together the hitherto-disparate history of Earth's near future. This would become more of a concern in the early 1970s, when the programme's reformatting meant that the majority of serials were set in the same notional near-future – though no one ever let continuity stand in the way of presenting entirely different Martians in 'The Ambassadors of Death' (1970), 'The Curse of Peladon' (1972) and 'Pyramids of Mars' (1975) or three varied destructions of Atlantis in 'The Underwater Menace', 'The Dæmons' (1971) and 'The Time Monster' (1972).

        Over the course of the tenures of Hartnell and Troughton, little was disclosed about the Doctor's background that had not been established in 'An Unearthly Child' (1963). In 'The Time Meddler' (1965), the Doctor runs into another exile from his home planet, the Monk (Peter Butterworth), a bumbling, cowardly, not-entirely-unsympathetic troublemaker who enjoys tinkering with Earth's history by importing pop-up toasters to the eleventh century. The Monk

The Doctor (Patrick Troughton) is forced to regenerate, 'The War Games'

returned as a secondary character, an on-off untrustworthy ally, in 'The Daleks' Master Plan', but was never heard from again. His manner, all fast-talking ingratiation and sudden mood swings, played well against Hartnell's sternness, but was too much like Troughton's Doctor for him to have made an effective antagonist in the later 1960s. With the Daleks established, the show looked for a human enemy, a Moriarty or Lex Luthor figure, to pit repeatedly against the Doctor. In 'The Celestial Toymaker', the Toymaker (Michael Gough), a being of transdimensional power, begins a contest which remains unresolved at the end of the serial. Despite a promise in the dialogue that the 'trilogic game' would be continued, the Toymaker never came back, though 'The Nightmare Fair' (scripted, but abandoned when *Who* went on a long hiatus in 1986) would have picked up this long-dropped thread. Human-seeming opponents like the Monk, the Toymaker and the Master of the Land of Fiction ('The Mind Robber') and disembodied entities like Morpho ('The Keys of Marinus', 1964), the Animus ('The Web Planet') and the Great Intelligence ('The Abominable Snowmen') proved the universe was scattered with individuals as high powered and formidable as the Doctor, or even far above him (albeit with flaws he could exploit). The Master (Emrys Jones), tired of his domain of the imagination, even saw the Doctor as a suitable replacement.

59

The series could probably have continued without revealing any more about the Doctor's origins, but the format was shaken up by a crisis that came at the end of the 1960s, when Troughton decided to move on and there was a feeling that perhaps the show had run its course. 'The War Games', a ten-episode epic (which dawdles in the middle), was scripted by Malcolm Hulke and Terrance Dicks as a culmination of the six-year story so far, climaxing in a shake-up that allows *Doctor Who* to regenerate for a new decade. The bulk of the serial concerns a planet where abducted human soldiers from throughout history play out their wars in separate zones as part of an unfeasible training exercise to create an army for use in galactic conquest. Among the humanoid villains behind this scheme is the War Chief (Edward Brayshaw), alien even to the race of abductors. His contributions to the war effort include the use of time–space travel boxes called SIDRATs. When the Doctor shows up and sabotages the games, the War Chief admits the interloper is a fellow Time Lord. This is the first mention of the race to which the Doctor and the War Chief, and presumably Susan and the Monk, belong. When the seriousness of the situation becomes clear to the Doctor, who cannot personally ensure the return of all the abducted Earthlings to their proper times, he overcomes obvious reluctance and summons the Time Lords. The final episode of 'The War Games' finds the Doctor dragged back to his as-yet-unnamed home planet.[22] We learn that he is not an exile (as Hartnell's Doctor claimed) but a renegade, who deserted 'an immensely civilised race' because he was bored.

The Doctor is put on trial for his various 'crimes' (starting with the theft of a TARDIS) and defends himself by counter-accusing that the Time Lords are a stifling society who refuse to do anything with their great powers (the Meddling Monk could have claimed this too). The Time Lords, swayed by testimony that the Doctor has done much good on his voyages, opt to punish him by forcing another change of appearance, removing the knowledge of how the TARDIS works from his mind and exiling him to the planet he has so often visited, Earth.[23] Whereas the regeneration of William Hartnell as Patrick Troughton was a spontaneous renewal that seemed a natural part of the Doctor's life-cycle, this metamorphosis is painful and forced on Troughton by the Time Lords. Jon Pertwee was not yet cast, so the Doctor is left in a state of howling flux at the end-of-season fade-out. Later regenerations are even more traumatic: Pertwee, Tom Baker, Peter Davison and Sylvester McCoy actually have to *die*, with much scenery-chewing and sobbing companions, before resurrecting in new bodies. Just once, the switch is surprisingly casual, in the Douglas Adams-scripted prologue to 'Destiny of the Daleks' (1979) where Romana tries out different bodies before settling on imitating a princess she met in 'The Armageddon Factor' (1979); this was a device to keep aboard the actress Lalla Ward, who guested alongside the original Romana, Mary Tamm.

The omniscience of the Time Lords is impressively established, and remote, patrician character actors like Bernard Horsfall (a frequent guest star) and Trevor Martin (who went on to play the Doctor in a stage production) convey an infinite superiority and jaded detachment that contrasts perfectly with Troughton's quixotic, sputtering Doctor, who is by contrast like a schoolboy dragged off a half-holiday and put in detention for playing conkers ('I expect they'll make me listen to a long boring speech about being a good boy. They like making speeches'). There is an echo here of a *Star Trek* episode, 'The Squire of Gothos' (1967), in which an all-powerful, swaggering alien humanoid (William Campbell) toys dangerously with Captain Kirk and his crew, but is revealed to be only a child, rebuked by far-more-evolved but notably-less-fun parents, two smug balls of super-intelligent life. Later – in 'The Deadly Assassin', 'The Invasion of Time' (1978), 'Arc of Infinity' and 'The Five Doctors' – the once-awesome status of the Time Lords will be reduced as it turns out that stay-at-home Gallifreyans tend to be corruptible incompetents liable to turn megalomaniac as soon as they take a place on the High Council. Other runaways (the Master, Morbius, the Rani) become the worst villains in the universe and even legendary Time Lord heroes like Omega end up threatening the fabric of everything. Though 'The War Games' establishes the Time Lords as non-interventionists who should at least have approved of preventing the Monk from changing the outcome of the Battle of Hastings, the trial sequence, in which the Doctor movingly defends his actions and Jamie and Zoe give testimony about the good he has done, seems to persuade them to amend the policy. 'We have accepted your plea that there is evil in the universe that must be fought,' he is told, 'and that you still have a part to play in that battle.'

61

The Doctor, summoning clips of monsters he has helped defeat, persuades the Time Lords that evil should be resisted; over the next few seasons, while the new Doctor is theoretically confined to Earth like a little boy sent to his room, the Time Lords are not above using their renegade to intervene discreetly in a variety of matters that would previously have been beneath them. The Master (Roger

Delgado), the next evil Time Lord to come along and theoretically a much worse baddie than the War Chief, never seems to attract the punishment dished out to the Doctor. By the time of 'Genesis of the Daleks' (1975), the Time Lords even want the Doctor (now Tom Baker) to violate what was previously their most sacred precept and alter history, whereupon – in another reversal – the Doctor has second thoughts and only half-changes the weave of history rather than wiping out the Daleks before they become a real menace. In *Doctor Who* (2005–), the Time Lords are supposedly gone, wiped out in a 'Time War' with the Daleks, though how a race with mastery of time travel *can* become extinct is still up for debate. The point of this is to dispense with a backstory that would be too cumbersome to reprise or revise while the show is trying to kickstart its own incarnation, while opening new mysteries about the Doctor's origins and recent activities still to be explored.[24]

Though the final episodes of 'The War Games' provide an answer to some of the ongoing mysteries, the Time Lords remain a paste-on solution which doesn't entirely fit what we were told earlier. They are so loftily powerful that it's hard to credit they couldn't track down the Doctor and his fugitive TARDIS before. Even if the random hops about time and space are interpreted as evasive action, the Doctor has become a big enough figure in the universe to attract attention; in 'The Chase', the Daleks – far less formidable than the Time Lords – locate and pursue the TARDIS. Later, in multi-Doctor anniversary specials, the Time Lords *are* casually able to scoop any of the Doctor's incarnations – *including* the First and Second versions – and summon them to dangerous missions. 'The Two Doctors' (1985), especially, is impossible to reconcile with 'The War Games'. There, Troughton is easily found by the Time Lords and sent on a mission. Writer Robert Holmes, who named Gallifrey and first explored its society in 'The Deadly Assassin', had forgotten it was the Pertwee Doctor who was at the beck and call of the Time Lords, whereas Troughton was supposed to be on the run from his race. Ironically, 'The Two Doctors' was made at a time when *Doctor Who* was especially concerned with its past – the serial brings back not only Troughton and Frazer Hines' Jamie, but the Sontarans, monsters Holmes had invented in 'The Time Warrior' (1974).

For the moment, the Time Lords are high-handed hypocrites, so detached and smug they only punish criminals who bother to turn themselves in. They return Jamie and Zoe to their own times, wiping from their minds all but their first adventures with the Doctor. This makes for one of the most poignant farewell scenes in the series, and seems especially callous in the case of Jamie – materialised during the massacre of rebel Scots inflicted by the Duke of Cumberland[25] and thus quite likely to be murdered within days. Since Zoe left her space station to learn from the Doctor, her character arc is rendered equally futile as any lessons are obliterated ('I just thought I'd forgotten something important, but it's nothing') and we assume she goes back to being a logician whose faith has just been shattered by the Cybermen. There is a concerted effort to recap and then dismantle the entire format. For the first of many times, montages of past monsters retrace the path that leads to this point. Then, all the givens of the show are altered or dispensed with: the Doctor, the companions, the TARDIS, the wanderings in time and space. It's now a commonplace approach – how many times were the X-Files shut down or shredded before a season-closing 'to be continued . . .' caption? – but was then genuinely disturbing, radical and unusual. Episode Ten of 'The War Games' ends with the Doctor spinning in darkness, one of the few cliffhangers in *Doctor Who*'s history that really does its job: left dangling, we really don't know what will happen next.

63

3 Invasion

The Third Doctor (Jon Pertwee) stumbles out of the TARDIS and collapses at the beginning of 'Spearhead from Space' (1970). He is rushed to a cottage hospital, where a cursory medical examination reveals that he has two hearts and an alien blood-type.

The Doctor's non-human status was a rarely addressed given on the show in the 1960s, arising only in his occasional telepathic bond with Susan and claims to be about 450 years old. As a plot function, his unearthliness only counted when he first regenerated and, finally, when he was tried by the Time Lords. Though several times under medical care – Hartnell goes to Tombstone in 'The Gunfighters' (1966) to have a toothache treated by Doc Holliday, and Troughton takes one of those sit-out-an-episode holidays in the sick bay of 'The Wheel in Space' (1968) – it had not before been established that he was physiologically distinguishable from an Earth-born human. From 1970 onwards, the Doctor's alien nature became more apparent, and would be stressed somewhere in almost every story. The revelation in *Doctor Who* (1996) that the Doctor is half-human was seen by many as a cop-out, but might serve to make him *more* alien, an outsider on Earth and among his 'own' people; in *Doctor Who* (2005–), he's back to being a complete alien, albeit one who sounds as if he's from Salford. Troughton replaced Hartnell with little fuss and not even a hiccough in the production schedule, but Pertwee – like all his successors — arrived after a great deal of publicity about 'the search for a new Doctor Who'. Before his debut, there was some question whether a performer best known as a 'funny voice' comedian on radio's *The Navy Lark* could handle the more serious sides of the Doctor, which perhaps prompted the sombre, 'adult' tone of his first season. In 1966, Troughton in 'The Power of the Daleks' followed Hartnell in 'The Tenth Planet' in the usual 'next week, another planet' course of a programme that was on for most of the year. After 'The War Games' (1969), *Doctor Who* was off the air for six months. When it returned in the first month of the 1970s, the face in the opening credits sequence was not the only difference.

Marooned on Earth by the Time Lords and bereft of travelling companions, the regenerated Doctor found himself a different man in a different show. But the character was also back where he was when we first met him. In 'An Unearthly Child' (1963), the Doctor had been settled in 1960s London long enough to send his granddaughter to school, and the TARDIS's wayward voyages brought him back to the present day as early as 'Planet of Giants' (1964). In 'The War Machines' (1966), *Doctor Who* first essayed a science-fiction/monster story with a contemporary British setting, as the Doctor (Hartnell) joins forces with the authorities to resist an out-of-control sentient computer and its cat's-paw military robots. During Troughton's tenure, monsters became an even more prominent feature of the series, and invaders (Cybermen, Ice Warriors) often menaced the Earth, usually in futures represented by unisex jumpsuits, silver-paper corridors and moon bases. However, 'The Evil of the Daleks' (1966) and 'The Abominable Snowmen' (1967), setting a precedent that would wear thin, have their villains arriving on Earth in the past: an English country house in 1866, Tibet in the 1930s. Humanity was threatened by so many alien invaders that 'Fury from the Deep' (1968) rings the changes by having the monster (sentient, mind-controlling seaweed) be terrestrial but inhuman, one of several *Who* species which emerge from the depths of time, the sea or the planet intent on taking over.

'The Web of Fear' (1968), a sequel to 'The Abominable Snowmen', and 'The Invasion' (1968), a (fairly) final defeat of the Cybermen,[26] develop the almost contemporary feel of 'Fury from the Deep'. The occasional video-phone nudges the setting a few months into

65

The Yeti, 'The Abominable Snowmen'

The Yeti, 'The Abominable Snowmen'

the future, but the high-street fashions and the weapons aren't from the *Buck Rogers* wardrobe raided for 'The Tomb of the Cybermen' (1967) or 'The Enemy of the World' (1967–8). 'The Web of Fear' introduces Major Lethbridge-Stewart (Nicholas Courtney), in command of the forces trying to clear the Yeti out of the London Underground. When the Doctor meets Lethbridge-Stewart again in 'The Invasion', he has been promoted to Brigadier (which is as far as he'll get) and is serving with the United Nations Intelligence Task Force (or Taskforce) (UNIT), an alliance of whitecoat boffins and tea-drinking British squaddies charged with defending the Earth against alien bullies. By the time of

The Doctor's second most-persistent foes, the Cybermen

'The Invasion', *Doctor Who* serials no longer stood alone, and back-references littered the scripts even as the production team attempted to reprise bits of business that had worked earlier. Written as a sequel to four earlier Cyberman stories and two Yeti attacks, 'The Invasion' also recalls performers who had been successful in other serials. The rich-voiced Kevin Stoney, memorable as the long-nailed quisling Mavic Chen in 'The Daleks' Master Plan' (1965–6), is cast in the similar role of Tobias Vaughan, a computer tycoon who initially allies with the Cybermen.[27] And the Cybermen's invasion of London, emerging from the sewers to strut around tourist landmarks, deliberately harks back to similar scenes in 'The Dalek Invasion of Earth' (1964).

In 'Spearhead from Space', the regenerated Doctor arrives on Earth almost simultaneously with a meteorite shower that turns out to be bringing the Nestene Consciousness – a malign alien entity with a plan to use the plastics industry to take over the country. Naturally, the Doctor wakes up to find the Brigadier on the scene and is co-opted to work with lady scientist Liz Shaw (Caroline John) against the Nestenes. The 1970 run of *Doctor Who* was more recognisable as a season than any previous span,[28] and instituted the BBC's policy of airing the show for six months, then taking a break until after Christmas. Without trips to other times or worlds, though there was a parallel Earth in 'Inferno', this season used the Doctor's frustration in exile (and at the mental blocks placed by the Time Lords) to make him a more peppery, even disagreeable character. Not since the early Hartnell days had the Doctor done anything like trying to run out in the middle of an alien invasion, which he does midway through 'Spearhead from Space'. The grown-up Liz and martinettish Brigadier don't fawn on the Doctor as younger companions had done; indeed, the Time Lord can't be a surrogate parent to them and sometimes takes the role of devious, naughty schoolboy to earn the Brigadier's moustache-bristling disapproval. Lethbridge-Stewart is even in a much-resented position of authority over his 'scientific advisor', and the warm relationship he had with Troughton's Doctor cools considerably. In 'Doctor Who and the Silurians' (1970), the Brigadier massacres a race of intelligent lizard-men

68

who want to reclaim the planet after millennia in hibernation and the Doctor is ashamed and disgusted – for the first time distancing himself from the violence and small-mindedness of humanity, a theme which will become more and more commonplace in the 1970s and beyond.

In the Doctor's frequent arguments with Lethbridge-Stewart, *Doctor Who* draws on *Quatermass and the Pit* (1959), in which the pacifist Professor Quatermass (André Morell) and military rocketry expert Colonel Breen (Anthony Bushell) are ordered to work together by the politicians. Boffin and Blimp repeatedly clash over general policy and specific decisions, and Quatermass is supported by Roney (Cec Linder), another humane scientist, just as Liz Shaw would take the Doctor's side in the many arguments that frankly padded out three of the 1970 serials to a hard-to-sustain seven episodes. Alongside basic debts to H. G. Wells' scientific romances, *Doctor Who* had always drawn on Nigel Kneale's *Quatermass* serials and John Wyndham's 'cosy catastrophes'.[29] 'Fury from the Deep', for instance, conflates the vegetable-human mutant of *The Quatermass Experiment* (1953) with the industrial location and mind-control elements of *Quatermass II* (1955) while stirring in the walking plant-life of *The Day of the Triffids* (1951) and the sea-dwelling, tendril-lashing evil intelligence of *The Kraken Wakes* (1953). The unique element is, of course, the Doctor. Wells, Kneale and Wyndham have their scientific, inquisitive heroes (and villains), but they tend to get involved in situations for professional or personal reasons; the 1960s Doctor just turns up in the middle of events and feels obliged to sort them out. After 'Spearhead from Space', the Doctor would become more like Quatermass, a government consultant.

Early 1970s *Doctor Who* dips time and time again into the Nigel Kneale back catalogue. The Nestene meteorites, familiarly known as 'thunderballs', are very like the pie-shaped stones, familiarly known as 'overshots', that split open to let free the invaders in *Quatermass II*.

69

The Autons, invaders with 1970s haircuts, 'Spearhead From Space'

The Nestene plan to substitute plastic doubles for high-ranking civil servants and other establishment worthies, not to mention their use of a factory as an Earth base, also derives from that serial. 'The Ambassadors of Death' (1970) has astronauts returning to Earth as zombified killers (actually, Martians in borrowed space suits), evoking the human–cactus hybrid of *The Quatermass Experiment*. 'The Dæmons' (1971) riffs on *Quatermass and the Pit* by opening at an archaeological excavation that turns up an alien spaceship in an ancient barrow and revealing that the persistent image of the horned Devil in human culture derives from an alien who arrived here a long time ago.[30] The influence extends even to *K-9 and Company* (1981) which, like 'The Dæmons', borrows its English village witch-cult from the Kneale-scripted Hammer film, *The Witches* (1968).

  Doctor Who was a voracious gobbler of ideas, often transforming generic material to its own ends. Elements from 'Mummy' films are recycled in 'The Tomb of the Cybermen', which even typecasts Hammer's high priest George Pastell (*The Mummy*, 1959; *The Curse of the Mummy's Tomb*, 1964), and 'Pyramids of Mars' (1975). However, the 1970 season drew on Quatermass not for one-use-only ideas and set-dressing but to create a format that was a template for a whole run of serials. Time and again, an alien threat in the English heartland would be resisted by military mobilisation and puzzle-solving scientists, and on-location sequences showed the terrified or bewildered public attacked by human-shaped monsters like the living shopwindow dummies of 'Spearhead from Space'. Kneale was not the only precedent for this version of *Who*. *Village of the Damned* (1960), from Wyndham's novel, *The Midwich Cuckoos* (1957), follows much the same course, though its plot has to develop over several years rather than the few hectic days of a typical Quatermass or Doctor Who adventure. Other low-budget British science-fiction films, themselves indebted to Kneale and Wyndham, also prefigure the UNIT years: *X the Unknown* (1958), *Unearthly Stranger* (1963), *The Night Caller* (1965), *Invasion* (1966), *Night of the Big Heat* (1967).[31] Specifics are carried over (like the alien barrier that seals off small communities in *Village of the Damned*, *Invasion* and 'The Dæmons') but the keynote is a general sense of muddling through by ingenuity and the poor bloody infantry, despite bureaucratic interference of the 'men from the ministry', that echoes a certain type of British war or peacetime crisis film (*The Small Back Room*, 1949; *Seven Days to Noon*, 1950).

UNIT was not the only scientific–military group working on television against alien invasion or other science-fictional troubles. Having shown the World Aquanaut Security Patrol (WASP) as our only line of defence against undersea tyrant Titan in *Stingray* (1964–5), Gerry Anderson developed the imaginary war theme in less whimsical manner with the non-acronymic but colour-coded SPECTRUM of *Captain Scarlet and the Mysterons* (1967–8) and the Supreme Headquarters Alien Defence Organisation (SHADO) of *UFO* (1970–3). Like the more earthbound UNCLE or even Maxwell Smart's CONTROL, SPECTRUM and SHADO were high-tech, multinational covert agencies (with independent television budgets large enough for a marketing-friendly array of gadgets and vehicles) and the Anderson shows followed their bitter secret wars against persistent alien invaders. On the BBC's licence-payers' money, UNIT couldn't compete with Anderson's wonderful toys. There were no die-cast Dinky models of the battered army lorries they trundled around in while Captain Scarlet zoomed off in a Spectrum Pursuit Vehicle. The colour-coded captains spent their off-duty hours in the luxury lounge of a floating city (Cloudbase) with the Angels, fighter pilots who could pass for fashion models, whereas the most Sergeant Benton (John Levene) and the UNIT lads could hope for was the odd cup of teabag tea brewed in a retort over a Bunsen burner by Jo Grant (Katy Manning) if she wasn't too busy getting into trouble.

In 'Spearhead from Space', the Brigadier tells Liz Shaw that UNIT has not only successfully resisted two alien invasions, but managed to keep the truth from the public – quite a feat, considering London was evacuated in 'The Web of Fear'. The Anderson shows assume cover-ups like these are a good thing, though *UFO* presents SHADO's near-totalitarian paranoia as not without human cost:

71

Commander Straker (Ed Bishop), head of the organisation, loses his wife (she thinks he's having an affair when he's only working round the clock to establish a line of defence against alien attack) and his son (Straker has to allot resources to tracking an alien invader rather than providing life-saving medical assistance). However, our viewpoint character in *Doctor Who* is the humane, sceptical Liz. She is immediately suspicious of the high-handed issuing of D-notices and cover stories, not to mention annoyed by the inconvenience of being seconded against her will from her academic research to join UNIT. By the time of *The X-Files* (1993–2002) and *Dark Skies* (1996–7), government anti-alien agencies are automatically suspect for their ruthless methods of ensuring panic doesn't spread among the public. An unproblematic good-guy force in the Troughton stories, UNIT became ambiguous in Pertwee's first season, with the Doctor often taking moral stands at odds with his notional employers. This strand culminates in 'Inferno', where the Doctor is shifted to a parallel reality police state.[32] In this fascist Britain, the Brigadier is an eye-patched hatchet man in the Republican Security Forces, usually cheery Sergeant Benton is a sadistic goon and even Liz a uniformed minion. When the Doctor returns to his reality after the alternate has been destroyed, he comments that the Brigadier too often reminds him of his evil doppelgänger.

In 1970, the certainties of 1960s science fiction were being questioned. The cynical, credible worlds of the detective show *Public Eye* (1965–75) and the spy series *Callan* (1967–72), which regularly exposed high-level corruption, opportunism and callousness, began to seep into the hitherto cleaner-cut universes of spacemen and aliens. Even the hawkish *Captain Scarlet* proceeded from a scenario whereby Earth started the war with the Mysterons when trigger-happy Captain Black destroyed their city on Mars. Kit Pedler and Gerry Davis, creators of the Cybermen, were behind *Doom Watch* (1970–2), a BBC programme in which a body of guilt-stricken boffins tries to police unethical uses of scientific advance – more often indicting political or business applications rather than science itself. The tension between the Doom Watch team and their political masters parallels that between Pertwee's

Doctor (backed by loyal assistants) and the Brigadier (and sundry politicians and generals) in early 70s *Who*. *Doom Watch*, given a 'serious, adult' 9.25 slot on Monday evening after the news, was more issue-led, though it perhaps remains lodged in the memory for imaginative, *Who*-like scare scenes as much as editorialising about pollution and genetic engineering.[33] Two weeks after 'Spearhead from Space' made chilling use of the plastics industry, with shopwindow dummies coming to life and attacking Ealing High Street, *Doom Watch* debuted with 'The Plastic Eaters', in which a virus engineered to biodegrade plastic waste gets loose on an aeroplane in flight to create another memorable nightmare sequence. *Doctor Who* came closest to *Doom Watch* with 'The Green Death' (1973), which touches on unethical big business, ineptly stored toxic waste and unemployment in the Welsh coalfields, as well as more traditional *Who* material like giant maggots and a megalomaniac computer. Jo Grant even defects from UNIT to join a hippie-ish commune who share the ideals of Doom Watch's Dr Spencer Quist (John Paul).

The two series echoed each other frequently. *Doom Watch* regular John Ridge (Simon Oates) is so worn down by two seasons of fruitless struggle that, in 'Fire and Brimstone' (1973), the third series opener, he uses phials of anthrax in an attempt to blackmail governments into revealing the extent of the environmental damage they are causing. *Doctor Who* regular Captain Yates (Richard Franklin), disenchanted with the modern world, joins Operation Golden Age, an ill-thought-through plot to undo the ills of the times by reverting to a pre-industrial society in 'Invasion of the Dinosaurs' (1974). In both cases, the reliable gimmick of a regular character going bad (like the constable revealed as corrupt on the cop show *Softly, Softly*, 1966–76) also gives a hitherto static sidekick role an 'arc' (a device not yet written into the scriptures of episodic TV writing). The disgraced Ridge has to leave Doom Watch and become a more committed advocate of the underdog in opposition to his officially neutral former boss Quist, while Yates's personal journey leads to a Buddhist retreat (and, indirectly, the Doctor's next regeneration) in 'Planet of the Spiders' (1974).

73

Doctor Who was more prone than Doom Watch to allegory: whereas the grown-up show tackled New Scientist headlines, the children's slot was likely to dress up issues as space opera. Even before the Doctor's exile was eased by the grateful Time Lords, when he teamed up with his former selves to save the universe from another renegade Time Lord in 'The Three Doctors' (1973), he was occasionally whisked off to other planets to intervene in situations that echoed 1970s concerns: capitalist exploitation of the third world ('Colony in Space', 1971), Britain's entry into the Common Market ('The Curse of Peladon', 1972), racist treatment of native peoples ('The Mutants', 1972), even a miners' strike ('The Monster of Peladon', 1974). This approach had been rare in the 1960s, despite occasional moral lessons like 'Galaxy 4' (1965) – where the beautiful Drahvins turn out to be baddies and the ugly Rills decent. The angry, occasionally earnest commitment of the Pertwee era mutated into the more cartoonish, satirical style[34] of later serials like 'The Pirate Planet' (1978), about galactic strip-mining, 'Warriors of the Deep' (1984), on nuclear stand-off (this was the year of Threads), 'Vengeance on Varos' (1985), about violent entertainment (finally answering Mary Whitehouse's criticisms), and 'The Long Game' (2005), about more trash television. Who went from non-committally predicting a near-future woman Prime Minister (in 'Terror of the Zygons', 1975)[35] through expressing the grumbles that led to Thatcherism in 'The Sun Makers' (1977), a whinge about income tax, to caricaturing the 1980s leaderine as Kara (Eleanor Bron) in 'Revelation of the Daleks' (1985), who simultaneously supports and plots the assassination of Davros in order to further her power plays, and Helen A (Sheila Hancock) in 'The Happiness Patrol' (1988), head of a totalitarian state which insists on the feelgood factor and uses a liquorice allsort killer robot to enforce a decree that everyone must smile.

The Doom Watch-like grimness of the 1970 Doctor Who season proved hard to sustain, and the format was modified in 1971. The bubbly Jo came on to replace the brainy Liz, the Brigadier turned

The Doctor's Moriarty, the Master (Roger Delgado)

75

comically phlegmatic ('chap with wings there ... five rounds rapid!') rather than genocidally ruthless and a token off-Earth serial ('Colony in Space') broke with a run of stories in which UNIT defended Shepherd's Bush. 'Terror of the Autons', the first serial of this batch, was – if anything – even stronger stuff than 'Spearhead from Space': it's the one with the fanged rubber imp doll, the killing plastic daffodils and the asphyxiating chair. Thereafter, however, monster-horror business was increasingly tinged with the surrealism and humour of pre-Pertwee *Who*: the colourful menaces of 'The Claws of Axos' are among the series' strangest invaders, and even the occult-tinged 'The Dæmons' has a creepy-funny cliffhanger which finds the Doctor threatened with ritual sacrifice by a troupe of evil morris dancers. The most important innovation was the introduction of the Master (Roger Delgado), a recurring villain who was mixed up in every story of the year. In the spirit of the mirror-image relationships of Holmes and Moriarty, Batman and the Joker or Professor X and Magneto, the Master was created as a near-even match for the Doctor. Another rebel Time Lord, but gloweringly evil, the bearded, Nehru-jacketed Master is similarly stranded on Earth and relishes teaming up with various alien or Earthly invaders. The Third Doctor's characterisation of the Master, in 'The Five Doctors' (1983), as 'my best enemy' is apt; as Mr Glass (Samuel L. Jackson) observes to the puzzled hero (Bruce Willis) in *Unbreakable* (2000), arch-enemies should be close and are often former friends.

The Master was a permanent addition. Delgado returns impressively in 'The Sea Devils' (1972), where he passes time in a Spandau-like prison by whistling along to the whimsical children's TV series *The Clangers* ('it seems to be a rather interesting extraterrestrial life form'). 'The Time Monster' (1972) and 'Frontier in Space' (1973) make less inspired use of the character, and Delgado's death in 1973 sidelined the Master. 'The Deadly Assassin' (1976) brings on a skull-faced Master (Peter Pratt) as the mystery villain behind a conspiracy against the Time Lords, lurking in the shadows of a serial which is concerned with filling in detail on the previously obscure world from which the Doctor and the Master came. 'The Keeper of Traken' (1981) was a more lasting reintroduction, concluding with the Master's disembodied spirit possessing the anagrammatical Tremas (Anthony Ainley). With Delgado-esque beard and a sneery laugh, Ainley played opposite four Doctors in the 1980s, killing Tom Baker in 'Logopolis' (1981) to bring on Peter Davison but appearing for the defence of Colin Baker in 'The Trial of a Time Lord' (1986). In 1996, the Daleks were merely mentioned in the *Doctor Who* TV movie, while Eric Roberts's Master sneered at Paul McGann. In 1999, Jonathan Pryce laughed maniacally at a succession of Doctors in 'The Curse of Fatal Death'. The fellow renegades frequently find themselves in temporary alliance against a monster of the month and work together better than the Doctor's multiple incarnations in the various team-up stories. Pertwee and Delgado enjoy witty exchanges that pass over the heads of the Earthlings around them, while Ainley mostly relishes the scenery he gets to chew and is even given fangs for that purpose in 'Survival' (1989).

As with the Daleks, progenitors of the successful Cybermen but also misfires like the Quarks and the Krotons, the Master worked so well that the series tried to develop similar but different troublemakers, starting with the booming mad (and, as it turns out, bodiless) former Time Lord, Omega (Stephen Thorne) in 'The Three Doctors'. Tom Baker, comical but not a comedian, preferred to bandy words with Basil Rathbone-like humourless fiends (Davros, Sutekh, Morbius, Weng-Chiang) until matched against chilly but wry one-off baddie, Scaroth (Julian Glover) in 'City of Death' (1979), allowing for a return of the Pertwee–Delgado style of verbal fencing. Kate O'Mara's Rani, teamed tetchily with Ainley in 'The Mark of the Rani' (1985), was a third rebel Time Lord (she, the Doctor and the Master were supposed to have been at university together), which made for amusing byplay in an otherwise duff serial. O'Mara stretched only to a single proper reappearance ('Time and the Rani', 1987), though she was the linchpin villain of the 3D multi-Doctor *Children in Need* charity crossover with *EastEnders*, 'Dimensions in Time' (1993). The most exciting concept for a Master-like villain, mishandled horribly in 'The Trial of a Time Lord', is the Valeyard (Michael Jayston), revealed as an evil future incarnation of the Doctor (somewhere between the twelfth and thirteenth regenerations), which takes the doppelgänger nemesis concept into areas the show never bothered to explore.[36]

77

Like many arch-enemy relationships, the Doctor and the Master settled into a grumpy rivalry that diminished dramatic impact. Holmes and Moriarty apparently killed each other in their *first* chronicled clash ('The Final Problem', 1893), but other arch-enmities tend to stretch over so many stories (and repeated failures to do away with hated opponents) that the initial effect is lost. At first, the point was to give the temporarily Earthbound show more impetus, propelling the enmity between serials. The Doctor, forced to live on Earth rather than given to dropping by every other serial, was becoming disenchanted with and intolerant of humanity, and the Master's sundry schemes gave him a personal reason to stick with UNIT. This also had the effect of making *Doctor Who* more soap-like, with separate serials but overarching plot threads, thus ensuring an audience's commitment to follow the whole show rather than dip in and out. For the first half of the 1970s, *Who* began each year with some sort of 'special event', publicised on a *Radio Times* cover, and intended to hook viewers for the season: a new Doctor ('Spearhead from Space', 1970), the arrival of the Master ('Terror of the Autons', 1971), the return of the Daleks ('Day of the Daleks', 1972), an anniversary get-together ('The Three Doctors', 1973). Note the change in emphasis from innovation to nostalgia, as the series starts to draw on its own past.

Even 'The Time Warrior' (1973–4), opener of Pertwee's final season (and the last *Radio Times* cover until 'The Five Doctors' in 1983), mixes shake-up (Sarah Jane replacing Jo, new alien villains in the Sontarans) with a revival of the historical settings fallen into disuse since 'The Highlanders' (1966–7). Robert Holmes' script takes the varied science-fiction-cum-historical mixes of 'The Time Meddler' (1965) and 'The Abominable Snowmen' – or those episode-long asides in time-and-space-spanning serials that find the Daleks on the *Mary Celeste*, in Ancient Egypt and a Victorian country house – and solidifies them into a formula (Earth's past threatened by alien time-meddlers) that could be recycled. This led to some of the best and best-remembered serials of Tom Baker's period, 'Pyramids of Mars', 'The Masque of Mandragora' (1976), 'The Talons of Weng-Chiang' (1977) and 'Horror of Fang Rock' (1978). The fact that 'Talons' ran straight into 'Horror' suggested this idea was being overplayed, especially since the wry Hammer pastiche of 'Talons' segued into the downbeat body count of 'Horror', in which the entire guest cast are killed off in a fogbound lighthouse by a malicious jellyfish creature (a Rutan) previously established as being in an endless war with the Sontarans. Nevertheless, the dead horse was flogged in the 1980s, in 'The Visitation' (1982), 'The King's Demons' (1983), 'The Mark of the Rani' (1985) and 'Ghost Light' (1989). Eventually, Sylvester McCoy found himself in a subset of meaningless runabouts set within living memory: 'Delta and the Bannermen' (1987), in a holiday camp in 1959, 'Remembrance of the Daleks' (1988), back in Coal Hill School in 1963 (an obvious riot of tied-off continuity), and 'The Curse of Fenric' (1989), during World War II. In the 2005 season, 'The Unquiet Dead', set in Victorian Cardiff, and 'The Empty Child'/'The Doctor Dances', set in the London Blitz, allow that alien encounters in the past are just an expected element of the formula; real resonance is saved for 'Father's Day', set in a year (1987) the script admits few time travellers would have any interest in visiting Britain.

The Doctor's exile was officially ended after 'The Three Doctors', but the format established in the UNIT–Master serials lingered, never quite fading away. Indeed, *Doctor Who* had been varying earthbound stories with outer space adventures even before the Doctor was allowed to remember how to operate the TARDIS. In 'Colony in Space', 'The Curse of Peladon' and 'The Mutants', the Time Lords despatch the Doctor on missions, using their tame renegade to intervene subtly in galactic trouble-spots. Only 'The Curse of Peladon' is a first-rate story, but these all further the more complex vision of human–alien relations that abounded in the 1970s, with Earth's interests often at variance with that of indigenes. 'The Mutants', the sort of story only possible in *British* science fiction, is set on the Earth colony of Solos in the thirtieth century, and features an independence movement, die-hard oppressors and a misunderstanding of the Solonian

'The Talons of Weng-Chiang'

79

life-cycle clearly analogous to racism. 'The Curse of Peladon' pulls a rare reversal by including Ice Warriors, the Doctor's Martian enemies, among a multi-species coalition visiting a mediaeval-level planet. The power-mad regime of 'The Ice Warriors' (1967) and 'The Seeds of Death (1969) has been succeeded by more reasonable government (rogue Martians are baddies again in the sequel, 'The Monster of Peladon'; *Star Trek: The Next Generation* (1987–94) would do something similar with the Klingons. By taking Jo along on these missions, the Doctor was harking back to the 1960s *Who* format. The deviousness of the Time Lords, who often manipulate the TARDIS without giving explicit instructions as to what the Doctor is supposed to do, means a certain mystery about where the Doctor makes planetfall that reintroduces some of the randomness of his earlier adventures.

'The Three Doctors' led directly into 'Carnival of Monsters' (1973), in which the Doctor again takes a random jaunt with an admiring sidekick, materialising in the middle of a trouble-spot without even a hint that the Time Lords are involved. As in 'The War Games' and 'The Android Invasion' (1975), 'Carnival' has the TARDIS turn up on what appears to be Earth (a ship in the Indian Ocean in 1926) but soon displays a wrongness (a time loop involving an attack by a sea serpent) which leads to the revelation that this is an artificial environment (within a machine that holds abducted specimens of many life-forms) on another world (the hidebound Inter Minor). 'Carnival', an excellent Robert Holmes script packed with ideas and witty footnotes, is significantly the first stand-alone *Doctor Who* serial since 'The Space Pirates' (1969), free of the Time Lords, UNIT and the Master, concerned just with being a good story on its own terms – though Ogrons (from 'Day of the Daleks') and a Cyberman are glimpsed as other species collected in the Miniscope. The Doctor and Jo proceed to hop around time and space for the bulk of the season, albeit tangling with old foes, the Master ('Frontier in Space') and the Daleks ('Planet of the Daleks', 1973), in what should be a two-serial, twelve-part epic but isn't. 'Frontier' ends with a fan-chilling alliance between the Master and the Daleks that goes nowhere and 'Planet' does not pick up from the revelation that the Daleks were the unseen force manipulating Earth and the Draconian Empire into a frontier war.

For the next three years, the TARDIS would touch base with Earth and UNIT about twice a season, initially in serials with 'significant' events like the writing out and bringing on of regular characters. Jo and the Third Doctor leave in 'The Green Death' (1973) and 'Planet of the Spiders' (1974), while Sarah Jane and the Fourth Doctor come on in 'The Time Warrior' (1974) and 'Robot' (1974–5) – which all feature the Brigadier, his soldier stuntmen and *Avengers*-like plot hooks involving scientists kidnapped to the past or a rogue robot. Though Jon Pertwee regenerated into Tom Baker, *Doctor Who* had no great format change in 1974. The mix of the later Pertwee seasons continued, with UNIT shows decreasingly apparent. After 'Terror of the Zygons' (1975), the Brigadier was dropped from the regular cast, replaced by one-off UNIT upper ranks in 'The Android Invasion' (1975) and 'The Seeds of Doom' (1976). Typical of *Who*'s tendency to make a fuss about beginnings but let endings peter out is the way UNIT was dropped: no big resignation scene or serial built around the Doctor's break with his former employers. The dangling thread would be picked up when Nicholas Courtney's Lethbridge-Stewart was brought out of retirement to support less popular Doctors in 'Mawdryn Undead' (1983) and 'Battlefield' (1989) and uniformed but uncharacterised UNIT brass are summarily murdered in 'Aliens of London'/'World War Three' (2005) to cut the Ninth Doctor off from anyone official who might believe in him. As it was, anyone following the overall story wondered why, dealing with trouble on contemporary Earth in 'The Hand of Fear' (1976) or 'Image of the Fendahl' (1977), the Doctor *didn't* wave his UNIT pass to get round obstructive officials.

When no one was sure how Tom Baker would pan out in the role, 'Robot' brought on a fresh male companion, Surgeon Lieutenant Harry Sullivan (Ian Marter), who travelled in time and space (though rarely in the TARDIS) with the Doctor and Sarah Jane. When it became clear that Baker had little need for a Jamie-like action-man sidekick, Harry was eased out. In his last serial, 'The Android Invasion', Marter appears mostly as an alien robot duplicate. Pertwee, expert in Venusian karate, see-sawed somewhat hypocritically between disapproval of the Brigadier's militarism and a take-no-prisoners attitude to alien baddies. After blowing up a Dalek in 'Planet of the Daleks', Pertwee declares 'You know, for a man who abhors violence, I took a great satisfaction in doing that.' Baker's Doctor was more likely to talk or scheme his way out of tight spots, offering jelly babies to humourless antagonists or tripping up guards with his trademark scarf. Bluff, bland Harry, a naval officer seconded to UNIT, was not quite enough of a contrast with this hero (he was even another doctor). To make much of the point, the Doctor needed to be partnered with someone whose attitudes were significantly different. Feral warrior Leela, a John Milius pin-up introduced in 'The Face of Evil' (1977) to replace Harry *and* Sarah Jane, has a tendency to slaughter enemies without mercy that allows the Doctor to be appalled and witty at the same time.

   This shift coexists with moments when the Doctor's alienness becomes more apparent. When the Doctor is too busy to grieve over a fallen comrade in 'Pyramids of Mars', an infuriated Sarah Jane accuses him of being 'not human' – a reminder that this is indeed the case. Fair enough, but just this once we sympathise with the shocked Sarah Jane who isn't too alienated to care about short-lived semi-comic characters like the just-killed Laurence Scarman (Michael Sheard). In 'The Brain of Morbius' (1976), Sarah Jane makes it clear that she preferred the Doctor when he was Jon Pertwee, and Tom Baker's pricklier Time Lord resents being reminded that he used to be 'sweet'. By the time Sarah Jane leaves, in 'The Hand of Fear', she is at the end of her patience. Distracted by an unprecedented summons to Gallifrey, the Doctor shoos her out of the TARDIS in what he confidently tells her is South Croydon – it turns out to be another entirely anonymous London suburb she'll presumably have to make her own way home from. The Third Doctor's thoughtful sulks about the rottenness of humanity give way to observations from Baker that come across like jokes, but emphasise his Doctor's inherent moral superiority. In 'The Invisible Enemy' (1977), the Doctor off-

handedly characterises mankind as a disease, then qualifies the insult with 'some of my best friends are humans [but] when they get together in great number other lifeforms sometimes suffer'. This isn't *quite* inconsistent with the characterisation in 'The Deadly Assassin' and 'The Invasion of Time' of his own people as corruptible, petty, fatuous and decadent – afflicted with supposedly typical human blights like political assassination, rigged elections, secret policemen and boring television commentators – since this Doctor has few illusions about the Time Lords either.

83

If 'Robot' was a shaky start to Tom Baker's tenure,[37] *Doctor Who* came back into focus with his second serial, 'The Ark in Space' (1975). As with many successful *Who* serials, 'The Ark in Space' – unconnected with the William Hartnell-starring 'The Ark' (1966) – brings on a fresh, original alien antagonist. The Wirrn are parasitical giant wasps who incubate in the cryo-frozen bodies of hand-picked humans awaiting the Earth's return to habitability after a solar flare, and the gruesome insect–human hybrid lurching around the satellite ark evokes the mutating astronaut of *The Quatermass Experiment* even as the set-up sketches an area of science fiction/horror that would achieve a much higher profile in the 1980s thanks to the many imitations of Ridley Scott's *Alien* (1979) and David Cronenberg's *The Fly* (1986). Unlike many successful monsters, the Wirrn did not return, so their initial impact hasn't been blunted through overfamiliarity (Daleks, Cybermen, the Master) or bungled handling by the inheritors of the concept (Sea Devils, Sontarans, Omega). Robert Holmes' script, reworking an idea by John Lucarotti, could as easily have been tailored to any of the previous Doctors, but the uncluttered first episode – which consists entirely of the Doctor, Sarah Jane and Harry exploring the space station – serves as a far more effective introduction to Tom Baker's reading of the role than the overly busy, deeply generic 'Robot'. Often, episodes which run heavily to wandering around corridors and ominous clues feel like padding; here, Baker develops his signature walk – hands in pockets, mobile neck, permanent semi-shrug – and the minutiae of his performance.

Baker's first season returned to wanderings in time and space, with the newly regenerated Doctor overcome by an urge to travel at the end of 'Robot'. The next four serials hooked together and three fell back on the audience-retaining insurance policy of returning to old enemies. After defeating the Wirrn, the Doctor hops down to the Earth of 'The Ark in Space' for the two-part 'The Sontaran Experiment', mostly to establish that the planet is habitable again, before being abducted by the Time Lords to tinker with continuity for 'Genesis of the Daleks' and returned to the Ark at an earlier period when the satellite was in use as a prosaic travel marker (the Nerva Beacon) for 'Revenge of the Cybermen'. Of these revivals, 'Genesis' is the most important and impressive. Terry Nation revisits the early history of Skaro, elaborating (and contradicting) backstory established in 'The Daleks' (1963) and giving the Doctor opportunities to intervene in the creation of the Daleks and (in a new form) rebel against Time Lord dictates. 'The Ark in Space', a pure horror story, was strong meat, but the downbeat 'Genesis', set on a planet degraded by an endless war between two totalitarian regimes, prompted angry letters to the *Radio Times* and was more responsible than any other serial for attracting the attentions of clean-up-TV campaigners like Mary Whitehouse. For children's programming, *Doctor Who* always had a high body count: UNIT troops were as expendable as *Star Trek* red shirts, popping off prop guns at implacably advancing monsters and then screaming as they were zapped or devoured. The seriousness of

84

Davros, creator of the Daleks

85

Nation's tone, and the depiction of a Doctor who could not make all Skaro's problems go away and was even unsure whether to try, made 'Genesis' a much rougher watch than the average *Who*.

Nation, eventual creator of the even more depressing TV science-fiction shows *Survivors* (1975–7) and *Blake's 7* (1978–81), had more on his mind than allegories of fascism, resistance, morality, societal collapse and renewal. In 'Genesis of the Daleks', he also had to make his pet creations scary again after they had been merchandised as plastic toys and become templates for three separate cake recipes demonstrated by Valerie Singleton on *Blue Peter* (1958–). This begins as Davros (Michael Wisher) unveils the first Daleks under the innocuous label of 'Mark III Travel Machines', ostensibly high-tech aids to those handicapped or mutated in the war. The cliffhanger of Episode One is not the Daleks' first murder, but an amendment: Davros adding a weapon to the design and announcing 'Now we can begin'. Throughout the serial, the Thal and Kaled factions of Skaro wipe each other out, with only the Doctor aware that the real danger comes from the almost-reassuring machines trundling off the production line in Davros's laboratory. The crux, in which the fate of the Daleks (and the universe) hinges on whether the Doctor touches two live wires together, is among the series' most often-excerpted moments, and revisits the conflict between meddling and non-intervention that always bubbles up at dramatic junctures. It is not only the Daleks being reinvented, but – four serials after regeneration – the Doctor. Troughton (and, by implication, Hartnell) fled from a powerful but detached society which *almost* never bothered with the business of lesser races; Pertwee followed orders, but bristled at lectures from a smug floating civil servant; but Baker has a *more* developed morality than even his own society. When a whole serial finally visits Gallifrey in 'The Deadly Assassin' (1976), we find out why.

Doctor Who had become more aware of its past, with elements of continuity accruing between regenerations and successful monsters rescued from supposedly final defeats to menace again, but 'Genesis of the Daleks' takes the show back to its roots even more radically than the chummy exercise of 'The Three Doctors'. Most stabs at 'significant' *Who* delve into the Doctor's still-mysterious past[38] but 'Genesis' revisits and rewrites the programme's universe. Some of its reimaginings would become encumbering in themselves: arguably, Davros should have been left dead and the use of quasi-religious titles for subsequent Dalek serials smacks of fannish pomposity. The overall seriousness of 'Genesis' carries over into 'Revenge of the Cybermen', which also brings back a once-overused menace (after a far longer hiatus) but stresses the Cyber race's diminished threat ('a pathetic bunch of tin soldiers skulking about the galaxy in an ancient spaceship'). Subsequent serials ('Earthshock', 1982; 'Attack of the Cybermen', 1985; 'Silver Nemesis', 1988) do little to make the Cybermen more formidable, consigning Troughton's most persistent foes to also-ran, not-as-nasty-as-Daleks status. In 'The Five Doctors', the Cybermen are just cannon fodder: the Master lets a whole troop get wiped out walking across a booby-trapped surface 'like sheep across minefields'. In 'Dalek'

(2005), a Cyber-head is mounted on display in a storehouse of alien bits and pieces, and Eccleston notes 'the stuff of nightmares reduced to an exhibit'.

The generally horrific, genuinely nightmarish feel of Tom Baker's first year on the show did not carry on, though the next two seasons represent the show's most sustained debt to horror as a genre since the run of 'scary monster' stories in the middle of Troughton's tenure.[39] 'Terror of the Zygons' was a Pertwee-style UNIT adventure set in the series' ongoing near-future Britain, but set a trend for co-opting established monsters (the Loch Ness Monster) into the world of *Who*. This was not unprecedented: the Intelligence of 'The Abominable Snowmen' dresses its robot minions up to evoke a pre-existing Earth legend (though a *real* Yeti appears at the end); 'The Dæmons' suggests alien intervention gave rise to human myths about demons and devils; and 'The Claws of Axos' was originally, bluntly called 'Vampire from Space'.[40] In short order, Tom Baker's Doctor encountered *Who* versions of Jekyll and Hyde ('Planet of Evil', 1975), the Mummy ('Pyramids of Mars', 1975), doppelgängers ('The Android Invasion', 1975), Frankenstein and his monster ('The Brain of Morbius', 1976), a killer plant ('The Seeds of Doom', 1976), Edgar Allan Poe's (and Roger Corman's) 'Masque of the Red Death' ('The Masque of Mandragora', 1976), the Beast with Five Fingers ('The Hand of Fear', 1976), the Phantom of the Opera/the Manchurian Candidate ('The Deadly Assassin', 1976), Agatha Christie's *Ten Little Niggers* ('The Robots of Death', 1977), a fogbound swirl of Fu Manchu, Jack the Ripper and a music-hall-inclined Phantom ('The Talons of Weng-Chiang', 1977) and a haunted lighthouse ('Horror of Fang Rock', 1977). 'State of Decay' (1980), *Who*'s inevitable vampire story, was commissioned from Terrance Dicks (as 'The Witch Lords') in 1977, during this sustained raiding of the gothic horror back-catalogue.

Though the series had hit on (another) formula for generating material, *Doctor Who* seemed at this point as capable of varying settings and subject matter as it had in the 1960s. Tom Baker's Doctor became more whimsical, impulsive and strange, but was not yet a pantomime caricature of his former self. Troughton's Doctor had been a master of non sequitur (his best-ever line reading is the shy, sly, indignant, irrelevant 'I like drawing pins' in 'The Space Pirates') and Pertwee could harrumph through red tape, but Baker's Doctor finally was a Time Lord, playing on a level far above anyone else around him. This was not someone who left Gallifrey because he was bored (when he goes back there, he finds endless ways to amuse himself by making fun of more pompous Time Lords) but because he thinks and feels too fast for any other life-form in the universe. He is unfazed when, in 'The Face of Evil', an entire planet believes him (with some justification) to be 'the Evil One' and merely offers his ever-present paper bag of jelly babies ('It's true then – they say the Evil One eats babies'). This Doctor, like this actor, is suited to being dropped in the middle of established stories because he enjoys playing in them – whether he is required to be Hercule Poirot, Sherlock Holmes,[41] a swashbuckling hero (*Who* did *The Prisoner of Zenda* in 'The Androids of Tara', 1978), Van Helsing or Quatermass. These horror skits are among the most *knowing* serials in *Who* history, too much fun to be *avant-la-lettre* postmodern and unpredictable enough to avoid the curse of campery which eventually fell (though 'Androids' is certainly among Baker's camper outings). They *are* scary, but with a wink: 'The Macra Terror' (1967) and 'Terror of the Autons' are seriously disturbing, full of characters who die screaming, but the Tom Baker-era spookshows have too much fun with the trappings of genre to be as ruthless.

A terileptil, 'The Visitation'

Haemovores, 'The Curse of Fenric'

By adapting other stories, *Doctor Who* could simultaneously exploit, homage and parody. When the Doctor interacts with Frankensteinian mad scientist Solon (Philip Madoc) in 'The Brain of Morbius' or plants-before-humanity lunatic Harrison Chase (Tony Beckley) in 'The Seeds of Doom', his carefree, amused, interested attitude points up the absurdity of the lunatic villain roles they are so intent upon playing. 'Morbius' deploys all the trappings of Universal–Hammer horror: a hunchback minion agitating for a new body, a patchwork creature rampaging around the laboratory, disembodied scheming brains (evoking Curt Siodmak's often-filmed *Donovan's Brain*), a gothic castle in a jagged landscape (here, an entire planet) lashed with storms, secret passageways and a sect of robed immortal priestesses worshipping an eternal flame which is guttering. In a satisfying joke that resonates all the way back to the first *Who* serial and its three episodes of stone-age scrabbling after 'the secret of fire', the Doctor solves the problem of the Sisterhood, reckoned even more powerful and wise than the Time Lords, by cleaning their chimney and relighting the flame. This may be Baker's finest moment as the Doctor, though as entire serials, the high-water marks of his tenure are the witty, creepy 'The Robots of Death', with its baroque androids and jaded human victims, and the spirited, action-packed 'The Talons of Weng-Chiang', which reveals that the disfigured Chinese fiend in the basement of a Victorian music hall is a time-travelling Icelandic war criminal from the far future.

4 State of Decay

Tom Baker was the longest-lasting Doctor (1974–81) and – not least because his shows have been more widely seen in the US than any other version of *Doctor Who*[42] – remains the performer most identified with the role. Audiences who came to the programme before 1974 had surprisingly little trouble accepting new Doctors, especially after it was established that changes would occur regularly. When he took the role, Baker was aware that 'no actor has ever failed in the part'; he survived a particularly weak first story, and his own initial over-reliance on Harpo Marxisms, to deliver outstanding work in an outstanding run of serials. Subsequent Doctors have been overshadowed by his tenure in the role, and arguably no actor since Tom Baker has truly succeeded in the part.[43] While Baker was the Doctor, the show's UK ratings improved, peaking around the middle of his run,[44] then declined to a point well below the figures of his predecessors. After Baker's departure, the show was shifted from its established time-slot to Tuesdays and Thursdays, then back to Saturdays for forty-five-minute episodes, then to mid-week again. Nothing really helped, and ratings remained iffy.[45]

     If Tom Baker's *Doctor Who* includes some of the show's best serials, it also runs to a great deal of the worst – 'Underworld' (1978), 'The Creature from the Pit' (1979), 'Nightmare of Eden' (1979), 'The Horns of Nimon' (1979–80), 'The Leisure Hive' (1980), 'Full Circle' (1980). If the Rolling Stones had died in a plane crash in 1972, they'd be remembered as a great band rather than tolerated as an embarrassing living fossil; and if the Doctor had not regenerated after being zapped by the Rutan on Fang Rock, Tom Baker really would be *the* Doctor. 'The Invisible Enemy' (1977), which immediately followed 'Horror at Fang Rock', is only below-par after a run of exceptionally fine serials. It returns to the sort of purely science-fictional settings rarely seen in Baker's first seasons – a hospital in space, along the lines of the backdrop for James White's *Sector General* novels. Like most of its immediate predecessors, the serial riffs on an established theme (miniaturised heroes explore a body as in *Fantastic Voyage*, 1966) and pops with ideas (some half-baked: the Doctor and Leela are reproduced as miniature clones to be injected into the disease-stricken Time Lord). It strikes me as the moment when *Who* jumps the shark,[46] mostly because it introduces K9, the chirrupy robot dog voiced by John Leeson (actually, only the first of several identical K9s). The immediate effect was to make *Who* seem much more a children's series than it had with Martian mummies, opium-addicted magicians or everyone in the lighthouse dying. Allegedly, the five-year-olds of 1977 loved K9,[47] but the five-year-olds of 1963 who had stuck with the show were mostly about to leave home and find other things to do with Saturday teatime.

Thanks to the imminent arrival of *Star Wars*, science fiction – at least as represented by film and television – was changing in 1977. K9 made his debut too early to be considered an imitation of R2D2, but he is one of a horde of allegedly cute robots – Twiki of *Buck Rogers in the 25th Century* (1979–81), *Metal Mickey* (1980–3), Muffit (another

K9 outdoors – rarely an effective effect

robo-dog) in *Battlestar Galactica* (1978–9), Bubo in *Clash of the Titans* (1981) – soon to become as obligatory as black precinct captains on American cop shows or camp gay best friends in films about neurotic single women looking for Mr Right. Rather than suggesting a policy of making *Doctor Who* 'more like *Star Wars*', K9's addition to the TARDIS crew reflects an unfortunate 'it worked once, so let's make it permanent' approach undone by the soon-to-be-obvious shortfall between what the writers asked of K9 and what the effects men could deliver. In theory, the robot dog was nearly as formidable as KITT of *Knight Rider* (1982–5), but in practice it was less manoeuvrable than a Dalek. In 'The Leisure Hive', K9 is sidelined for a whole serial (as was often the case) after trundling into the sea and short-circuiting while playing fetch with Romana on Brighton beach. The scene feels like the production team's revenge on a recalcitrant prop: a promised remote-controlled K9 couldn't cope with shingle and had to be pulled along on a string. 'A Girl's Best Friend' (1981), the *K-9 and Company* pilot, cruelly exposed the problem that the dog couldn't actually *do* anything much.

'The Invisible Enemy' was followed by 'Image of the Fendahl' (1977), a last gasp for *Doctor Who* as a scary show. Whether the programme had played out this string as far as possible ('Fendahl' goes back to the Nigel Kneale well once too often) or was bending under pressure from those who always deemed it 'too violent' or 'too frightening' for children (complaints rarely heard *from* children) is moot. The move away from *Who*-as-horror need not have been a disaster. A frequent complaint from science-fiction readers is that TV and film science fiction tends to be horror in disguise, the approach that would eventually lead to the *Who*-influenced *Alien* (1979). Kneale had made a virtue of this genre-scrambling, setting a pattern that *Who* followed, especially in the late-1960s and the mid-1970s. An apotheosis of black-and-white gothic science fiction came in the first season (1963–4) of *The Outer Limits*, but there were many less sophisticated, monster-of-the-week efforts (e.g.: the parade of mummies, werewolves, Yeti, evil puppets, plant-men and ghosts that invade the *Seaview* on

93

Voyage to the Bottom of the Sea, 1964–7). *Star Wars* broke the inevitable yoking of science fiction and horror, only to replace it with an equally inevitable yoking of science fiction and heroic fantasy. Dressing up leftovers from Hollywood Westerns and war films or big fat fantasy trilogy paperbacks in science-fiction guise, *Star Wars* effectively squeezed science fiction out of its own genre, a course subsequent TV and film science fiction has generally tended to be happy to stick with.

Terry Nation's *Blake's 7* (1978–81) was the BBC's attempt to cash in on *Star Wars*, put in development when George Lucas's film was an unknown quantity: it's a grim space opera, an anti-*Star Trek* on a *Who* budget. Curiously joyless and soapy, *Blake's 7* was perhaps the perfect show for its depressing times, but it prompted *Doctor Who* to lighten up by way of counter-programming. *Who* had always thrived on format changes, and 'The Sun Makers' (1977) seems a viable non-horror direction for the show. The Doctor and Leela find the planet Pluto has been terraformed and is run by a company which murderously exploits and literally overtaxes its workforce, and all the world's ills are caused by a profiteering fungus. Tom Baker's increasingly self-aware, jokey Doctor was suited to satirical adventures in Swiftian worlds which were at once fantastical and representative of human failings. It could be argued that *Who* was pillaging *another* strain of Nigel Kneale's work, the dystopian satire of his adaptation of *Nineteen Eighty-Four* (1954)[48] and the original TV plays *The Year of the Sex Olympics* (1968) and *Wine of India* (1970). This approach, followed intermittently for the rest of the series' run, never quite took. A certain smugness makes the Doctor's struggles with oppression seem pat: stories like this work best with *complicated* cartoon villains, not hissable pantomime baddies. The need to overthrow oppressive societies in final episodes to provide happy endings is also at odds with the inherent pessimism of the dystopian subgenre. The 1977–8 season, with K9 still trundling and chirruping, wound down with 'Underworld', one of several myths-in-space exercises, and the protracted 'The Invasion of Time' (1978), a Gallifrey serial that goes over the material of 'The Deadly Assassin' (1976). The season finale protracted itself by bringing back the

94

Sontarans for the last two episodes and had to palm off Leela in a suddenly arranged marriage to get Louise Jameson out of the show.

For the 1978–9 season, *Doctor Who*'s big idea was to string six stories onto an overall plot – which actually owed a lot to 'The Keys of Marinus' (1964), in which four keys had to be found in different locations on a planet within six episodes. In the 'Key to Time' arc, six segments of the MacGuffin are scattered throughout time and space disguised as various items; the Doctor, now partnered with a junior Time Lady Romana (Mary Tamm), has to collect the full set, with one piece picked up in each serial. The individual stories are a mixed bag, but none are especially inspiring. It was during this period that *Who* fans complained that it was becoming too much of a piss-take of itself; though it is probably more telling that it was during this period that fewer people who weren't *Who* fans were actually watching the programme. Actually, the problem is not so much that the show was funny but that it tried to be funny far more often than it succeeded. Douglas Adams' later spell as script editor and occasional writer meant an influx of witty lines and situations, but much of the humour was feeble. Jokes about the Doctor's age, unlikely alien customs or encounters with famous historical characters had worn thin by the early 1970s, and tended by now to be real groaners. The whole 'Key to Time' business, with the Doctor caught between representatives of Good and Evil who turn out to be two sides of one being, hamstrung individual serials with the continuing thread and inevitably paid off with an anticlimax. The enormously powerful object (something along the lines of Marvel Comics' Cosmic Cube or Infinity Gauntlet) is assembled and then thrown away because, after picking up all the pieces, the Doctor decides the thing is too dangerous and gets rid of it.

95

After that, it was time to fall back on a tactic that had often served – reviving an element of the original 1963 premise. At the end of 'The Armageddon Factor' (1979), the Doctor activates the TARDIS's 'randomiser circuit' so that it will hop about unpredictably in time and space to avoid the Black Guardian (Valentine Dyall), though when that villain tardily attempted revenge in a trio of 1983 serials he had little

Tom Baker, Mona Lisa,
Lalla Ward, 'City of Death'

trouble finding the now-regenerated Time Lord. To begin the 1979–80 season, *Doctor Who* trotted out the Daleks (and Davros) again for 'Destiny of the Daleks' (1979), then followed through with 'City of Death' (1979), the most successful of the show's attempts at reasonably sophisticated humour (signalled by cameos from John Cleese and Eleanor Bron). 'City of Death' proves that as late as 1979, *Who* could make a comical approach work *for* the show rather than undermine it. Sadly, the next three serials are ramshackle nonsense that do nobody any favours. The most notable collateral victim of this duff stretch was Lalla Ward's second Romana. Given good material, she was one of the most appealing regulars the show ever had; sadly, she was more likely to be stuck with the weakest scripts, Baker's least-committed performances, the recalcitrant K9 and wretched, baggy rubber-suit monsters (the Mandrels, the Nimon). It's no surprise half as many people were habitually watching the show as two years earlier.

John Nathan-Turner, *Who*'s producer from Baker's final season (1980–1) to the show's cancellation in 1989, tried to halt the drift towards lazy self-parody, reining in the star's improvisation, writing out K9 and upping middlebrow science-fiction content. If anything, however, Nathan-Turner's first season was duller even than departing producer Graham Williams' last, distinguished by more rubbish monsters (the Foamasi, Meglos) and the awkward introductions of *three* childish new companions and Anthony Ainley as the Master to carry the show over into the next Doctor. 'Full Circle', the tardy vampire serial 'State of Decay' (1980) and 'Warriors' Gate' (1981) form a trilogy only by virtue of being set in 'E-Space', a section of the universe that seems no different from anywhere else but which the scripts make a fuss about. Nathan-Turner set up a *proper* trilogy in 'The Keeper of Traken' (1981), 'Logopolis' (1981) and the next season's 'Castrovalva' (1982), an arc about the Master's return and his murder of the Fourth Doctor, bringing about Tom Baker's regeneration into Peter Davison. Uniquely, 'Castrovalva' is a post-regeneration serial in which the Doctor's adjustment to his new identity is the main thrust of the story rather than a subplot. The regeneration premise was refined to suggest that each incarnation of the Doctor actually *dies* before the next (seen first as a hovering ghost figure) melds with his corpse to become a new being.

Nathan-Turner set in stone elements that would make 1980s *Doctor Who* hard to watch and many commentators regard him as a greater wrecker than K9 and Michael Grade combined. The first four Doctors had a *style*, but not a specific costume: when in Tibet, Troughton wore a shaggy fur coat, for instance; and even Pertwee had a wardrobe of *different* frilly shirts, velvet jackets and caped ulsters. From the middle of Tom Baker's tenure, each Doctor unvaryingly sports their own distinctive, question-mark-pocked uniform as if dressing up as themselves. It's a comic-book convention, unsustainable in live-action where audiences wonder if the hero is indeed wearing the same, never-cleaned, never-worn-out clothes for years on end. The colourful, garish look of Nathan-Turner's Doctors (most appallingly Colin Baker) carried over into sparkly art direction that tended to make futuristic or alien societies seem like forgotten corners of a children's variety show, as did a tendency – once Tom Baker was gone – to cast familiar faces and names much as Morecambe and Wise used to rope in slumming stars for their skits. Until 1980, the typical *Who* guest star was a solid character actor like Michael Gough, Marius Goring, Philip Madoc, Kevin Stoney, Bernard Horsfall, John Bennett or Julian Glover, enjoying themselves but bringing a certain gravitas to mad scientists, universe-conquerors or

insidious fiends; thereafter, the show tended to get 'turns' from Beryl
Reid, Alexei Sayle, Richard Briers, Ken Dodd, Nicholas Parsons or
Gareth Hale and Norman Pace, who could tell their kids they'd been on
Doctor Who but hardly attempted acting.[49] Other obvious and intrusive
elements were jangling electronic music, the phasing out of filmed
inserts in favour of flatly shot, outside broadcast video, shrill
companions representing a middle-aged fantasy of 'young people' and
endless attempts to fold the show in on itself by evoking its past.

     Though blander than his predecessors, Peter Davison did a fair
job in his first season and his freshness shook up the format even as
Doctor Who was marooned in an uncongenial twice-a-week-on-a-
weekday evening slot which broke with its traditional Saturday teatime
home and exposed its increased childishness to a theoretically more
adult audience. There were dead losses like 'Four to Doomsday' (1982)
and 'Time-Flight' (1982) and the over-reliance on old enemies began

The Doctor (Colin Baker)
practically begging for
cancellation

with the Cyberman serial 'Earthshock' (1982), but Christopher Bailey's 'Kinda' (1982) is one of the series' best scripts. Set on a paradise planet where colonial exploiters tend to go mad, 'Kinda' eerily uses the show's limbo status between adult and children's programme by disturbingly having grown-up characters under an alien influence act like kids and tackling serious political and religious issues without becoming cartoonish or hectoring. Even Adric (Matthew Waterhouse) and Tegan (Janet Fielding) become more complicated characters: Adric, one of those boy geniuses who never win friends on science-fiction TV (eg: Wesley on *Star Trek: The Next Generation*, 1987–94), is here half-clever, panicky and often-pathetic just like a *real* smart kid, while Tegan gets to be inhabited by ultimate evil for a while but also to have a rare moment of grown-up sexuality with the bare-chested native prince who passes on the possessing snake-God with a touch. The Doctor consults a wise woman (Mary Morris) who labels him an idiot ('I have been called that, many times'), which prompts him to take a humble, quizzical, involved, sensible but wry approach to the situation that puts clear blue water between this Doctor and any of the others.

99

After the written-by-numbers aliens-in-history effort 'The Visitation' (1982), in which Terileptils start the Great Fire of London, came another sprightly, promising effort, the two-episode holiday 'Black Orchid' (1982). For once, the Doctor and friends are allowed to turn up (in a Wodehousian 1925 of cricket and country-house weekends) and have a good time at a party for a whole episode before a monster (a disfigured son thought dead after torture in the Amazon) escapes from the attic and the Doctor is framed for murder. Sometimes cited as a return to the historical stories of the Hartnell days, this has as much in common with the redressed horror stories of Tom Baker's era (it derives partly from *The Oblong Box*, 1969), but is also a refreshing change – not least because it gets Janet Fielding and Sarah Sutton out of unflattering 1982 costumes and into 1920s masquerade frocks which now look far more appealing. Here, the perennially sulky Adric is used for comic relief, the subject of sisterly teasing about his scoffing at a buffet ('I didn't have breakfast'). With 'Kinda' and 'Black Orchid', *Who* seemed on the point of a genuine revival and Davison had found a performance. Tom Baker's Doctor had become more Time Lordly and arrogant, but Davison's youthful, cricket-togged fellow was less instantly judgmental, intent on inspiring enemies (often misguided rather than evil) to question their own actions and tolerant of sidekicks Baker would have gleefully booted into the time-stream.

However, it didn't last. Instead of delivering more serials as good as 'Kinda', the next season simply did a copycat sequel, 'Snakedance' (1983). The remainder of Davison's tenure found *Doctor Who* obsessively bringing back not only the Daleks ('Resurrection of the Daleks', 1984) but other foes and friends, like Omega ('Arc of Infinity', 1983), the Black Guardian (three serials in 1983), the Master (five times) and the Brigadier ('Mawdryn Undead', 1983). In the Pertwee era, the prehistoric lizard men of 'Doctor Who and the Silurians' (1970) were followed by their undersea cousins in 'The Sea Devils' (1972); in 'Warriors of the Deep' (1984), these long-forgotten races form an alliance, represented by shoddier costumes and make-up, and *Who* essentially sank to doing its own fan fiction. The most extreme example is the 'anniversary special', 'The Five Doctors'[50] (1983), which recalls Patrick Troughton and Jon Pertwee, acceptably recasts Richard Hurndall as William Hartnell, uses footage from the unaired and incomplete 'Shada' (1980) to represent Tom Baker, finds roles for a clutch of former companions (even props like Pertwee's vintage car, Bessie), makes yet another trip to Gallifrey to find a Time Lord official gone bad, and incidentally features a Dalek, some Cybermen and a Yeti (and bloody K9). Amazingly, Davison and his current companions get a look-in too. 'The Three Doctors' (1973) managed to be significant in the evolution of the series at the time, but 'The Five Doctors' is just a celebratory runabout along the lines of the charity skit 'Dimensions in Time' (1993). Every time we learn more about Time Lord history (and the much-evoked founder of the race, Rassilon) it gets less interesting, and faces from the past pop up for nostalgia rather than to do anything with their characters.

Colin Baker and Sylvester McCoy need not trouble us long. Peri (Nicola Bryant), of the cleavage and shaky American accent, was introduced in 'Planet of Fire' (1984) to partner the Doctor into his fifth incarnation, loitering around with Davison into his final serial, 'The Caves of Androzani' (1984), which ended with his Doctor's death and regeneration into Colin Baker ('and not a moment too soon'). As with quite a lot of 1980s *Doctor Who*, there was a workable idea behind Baker's Doctor – after the kind, sensitive, humane, questioning, feeling Davison, Baker came on as rude, brusque, arrogant, lofty and know-it-all. Of course, as with the crotchety Hartnell, he settled down to be a universe-saving hero – but he started out trying to throttle his companion and ranting like a maniac. In an attempt to kickstart the new regeneration, Baker's first serial was tagged on to the end of a Davison season before the show took a break and returned back to its old Saturday slot but at a forty-five-minute length which had been experimented with for 'Resurrection of the Daleks' and would become standard (though still problematic) by the time of *Doctor Who* (2005–). It didn't help that 'The Twin Dilemma' (1984) was a feeble story with ugly sets, weak guest cast (Maurice Denham honourably excepted), a ludicrous monster (a giant slug played by the unfortunate Edwin Richfield) and an excess of pointless running around. Coming immediately after 'Planet of Fire', with a location jaunt to Lanzarote, and 'Androzani', which at least ran to caves, 'The Twin Dilemma' looked especially cheap and tacky, as if the hideous design of the Doctor's parti-coloured outfit infected the rest of the production. Of course, this Doctor was supposed to be tasteless and unpleasant – but that didn't mean the show ought to be. This Doctor's coat seemed to consist of strips from the costumes of all the previous incarnations sewn together – and too often so was Baker's performance.

101

The Sixth Doctor was around for two abbreviated seasons, with a lengthy hiatus as the BBC considered discontinuing production. Looking again at the 1985 serials, it's easy to sympathise with Michael Grade. As an audience insurance policy, the season began and ended with perennial foes, 'Attack of the Cybermen' and 'Revelation of the Daleks', tentpoling in the middle with 'The Two Doctors', which teams Baker with Troughton. Each fifty-minute episode drags, with a surfeit of

'Blatantly phallus-faced', a Vervoid from 'The Trial of a Time Lord'

the corridor-running business that pads out even some of the best *Who* serials and the odd interesting bit of business ('Vengeance on Varos' has the most of these) swallowed by the sort of silliness you might expect of a matinée pantomime which isn't going well, encouraging everyone to desperate, self-loathing ad-libs. The 1986 season consisted of 'The Trial of a Time Lord', which contains three four-part serials and two wrap-up episodes. The Doctor is (again!) tried by his own people, prosecuted by his evil future self (Michael Jayston's Valeyard). Three blah, archetypal adventures are shown, notable mainly for the most blatantly phallus-faced monsters in the series' history (the floral Vervoids), while the frame story continually falls down with its poorly written courtroom scenes (a running joke has the Doctor address the prosecutor as 'the Boatyard', 'the Scrapyard' and variants). The series gets shot of Peri in an amazingly unpleasant manner: she gets tortured by the Doctor, has an evil alien personality imprinted over her own and is killed by barbarian King Yrcanos (Brian Blessed at his shoutiest), though presumably her mind was destroyed before her bald body. On second thought, this is taken back (she gets better or the visual testimony was a lie, and marries Yrcanos), by which time she's been replaced by a companion even *Who* fans found hard to warm up to, Mel (Bonnie Langford).

Oddly, Langford returned next season but Baker was unceremoniously kicked off the show. This behind-the-scenes business

Bonnie Langford!

Kate O'Mara doing Bonnie Langford

103

means 'Time and the Rani' (1987) opens with the most perfunctory regeneration in *Who* history. Before the credits, the TARDIS is buffeted about a bit and the Doctor falls over, a glow superimposed on his face to conceal the fact that he's Sylvester McCoy in a wig and Colin Baker's horrible coat. Like Colin Baker, McCoy has the makings of a fine Doctor but had the misfortune to be cast when the series had run low on inspiration, shucking off so many identities and formats that it could only cobble together scraps of its past to limp through seasons. His best performance in the role, sadly, comes in the pre-Paul McGann scenes of *Doctor Who* (1996), where he plays up an interesting out-of-time melancholy. McCoy's slight Scots burr highlights the paradox that all the earlier Doctors are at once alien beings from Gallifrey and somehow *English*. McGann is even asked if he's British and muses 'Yes, I suppose I am.' The ethnicity of aliens is always complex. In America, a British accent often signifies otherworldliness, as with Klaatu (Michael Rennie) in *The Day the Earth Stood Still* (1951) or Thomas Jerome Newton (David Bowie) in *The Man Who Fell to Earth* (1976). In British science fiction, this has less weight: it follows that casts are almost exclusively from the country where a film or TV show is made.[51] All the Time Lords and Ladies of *Doctor Who* have been fussy, eccentric British character actors, but until McCoy they also had modified RP accents, which makes the question of where this Doctor's 'educated Scots' tones come from vexed. In 'Rose' (2005), the heroine (Billie Piper) asks the Ninth Doctor (Christopher Eccleston) why, if he's an alien, he has a Northern accent and is told 'lots of planets have a North'. The Tenth Doctor (David Tennant) reverts to Anglicised Scots, and – in his first moments in 'The Parting of the Ways' (2005) – is briefly fazed that regeneration has rearranged his teeth, suggesting *some* rationale for the vocal variances.

    Doctor Who was probably terminal when McCoy was cast, but lingered for three seasons of four serials apiece before the series that began with 'An Unearthly Child' (1963) ended with 'Survival' (1989). The scaling-back of production meant more three-episode serials, though they still seemed as padded and given to silly dashing around as many a six- or seven-parter of earlier years. McCoy was permanently clamping his panama hat to his head so it wouldn't blow away while he was chased, and made as emphatic use of his question-mark-handle umbrella as the Penguin. As with Colin Baker, he was especially likely to get stuck with feeble cliffhangers and silly escapes: in 'Dragonfire' (1987), he even climbs over the edge of a cliff for *no reason other than to hang there* by that umbrella at the end of one episode, only to notice at the beginning of the next that there's a handy ledge which means he won't plunge into the bottomless abyss. During McCoy's tenure, *Who* continued its revival policy by bringing back threadbare old favourites, the Cybermen in 'Silver Nemesis' (1988), the Brigadier and UNIT in 'Battlefield' (1989) and the Master (now with fangs and yellow eyes) in 'Survival'. 'Remembrance of the Daleks' (1988), the most elaborate of these fanfic exercises, is even set in 1963, and has Daleks invading Coal

Hill School, with a subplot about yet another all-powerful artefact ('the Hand of Omega') from Time Lord history and the revelation that Davros (Terry Molloy) *is* the Emperor Dalek (or at least his living severed head is inside the carapace). Even more typical is the exceptionally tardy and laboured follow-up to *one line of dialogue* in 'Planet of the Spiders' (1973) which suggested the Brigadier had spent a dirty weekend in Brighton with a woman named Doris; sixteen years later, 'Battlefield' made an honest woman of this once-mentioned, never-before-seen character by establishing that the now-retired Lethbridge-Stewart has married her (Angela Douglas).

More distinctive, in that they try to address the late 1980s rather than evoke baby-boom nostalgia, are a run of studio-bound satires, 'Paradise Towers' (1987), 'Dragonfire', 'The Happiness Patrol' (1988) and 'The Greatest Show in the Galaxy' (1988). If *Who* has turned into a pantomime, these at least try to make a point of the style, with enclosed, artificial settings, black humour (sweet little old lady cannibals, cheerful pink-swathed death squads), in-jokes (characters named after film theorists, a fan of the Greatest Show in the Galaxy who rants like a stereotype *Who* anorak) and villains who stand in for real-world hate figures (an architect who can't bear people living in his perfect buildings and so riddles them with death traps, the Thatcherite leader of the Happiness Patrol). Too often, stretches of sharp writing are undone by lax plotting, variable performances and hurried direction, but McCoy shows real spirit, even if he does come across as a 1980s alternative comedian in space. His Doctor is a busker (his instrument seems to be the spoon) who draws a crowd with patter and some gags, then lectures them about the miners' strike or council house sell-offs. His finest moment comes in 'Battlefield', in a confrontation with an unusually shaded incarnation of evil, Morgaine (Jean Marsh), as he convinces the extradimensional witch woman that her entire worlds-spanning war with the dead King Arthur has been a lovers' spat and that, though she adores battle and martial pageantry, triggering World War III on Earth is too appalling even for her. The scene has been set up by Morgaine's genuinely alien priorities – she uses her magic casually to

105

kill sympathetic characters but pays for a round of drinks in a pub by curing the landlady's blindness – but McCoy's passion makes it work; how typical that it leads into one of the show's most feeble anticlimaxes, as Morgaine is arrested and glumly hauled off to prison.

With the likes of Richard Briers, Sheila Hancock, Anton Diffring, Sylvia Sims and Ronald Fraser cast as elder generation baddies, the McCoy serials side with equally parodic yoof characters like the girl gangs of 'Paradise Towers' or the punky troupe (including a spiky werewolf chick) of 'The Greatest Show in the Galaxy'. For the first time since the 1960s, the companions were consistently treated as viewpoint characters rather than tagalongs. Hands-on-hips principal boy Bonnie Langford was whisked off and replaced by Sophie Aldred's overbearing Ace, who at least had a funny backstory: a school-leaver stuck with a boring job as a fast-food waitress in Perivale, Ace wished for a life of adventure out in the wide universe and was transported to the fabulous Ice World only to get stuck with essentially the same boring job in an alien fast-food joint. There was an attempt to make the Doctor more mysterious (mostly throwaway lines) by shifting the attention to Ace, who had a character through-line in the last three serials in 1989, 'Ghost Light', 'The Curse of Fenric' and 'Survival'. The initial tendency to have Ace as a cringeworthy character (always bellowing 'wicked', 'brill', 'mega' or, indeed, 'ace') was never quite exorcised, and those last stories are crippled by scripts that trot out a great many ideas, themes, characters and settings but seem to have no idea at all about turning promising elements into narrative drama.

In its final season, *Doctor Who* could still deliver surprising scenes amid the incoherent mediocrity. Aside from Jean Marsh's Morgaine, the best thing on the show in 1989 is Katharine Schlesinger, in male evening dress, singing 'That's the Way to the Zoo' in the Victorian-set 'Ghost Light'. The actress's attack illuminates the murkily developed evolutionary theme of the serial and suggests steel under prettiness that hints at a character development which is then lazily bungled. Strangely, one element which had declined over the decades made a final comeback: the monsters. After ten years of the baggy likes of the Nimon, the Myrka and the Vervoids, *Who* began to make men-in-suits creatures or use special effects make-up in a way fans didn't need to apologise for. Sadly, the programme rarely had its most impressive creations – the demonic Destroyer of 'Battlefield', the barnacled aqua-vampire Haemovores and Hammer-look Twins of Evil of 'The Curse of Fenric', the cheetah people of 'Survival' – do anything more terrifying than linger in the shadows or advance menacingly.

Endings are tricky, and *Doctor Who* ceased production without the benefit of enough advance notice to prepare the kind of final lap most shows try for. Dr Kimble cleared his name, Bob watched the army lorry drive off with Terry, the M*A*S*H unit came home from Korea (where they'd been four times as long as the war), Blake's Seven were shockingly wiped out (you expected a happy ending?), the Crossroads motel burned down, Inspector Morse and Victor Meldrew died, Diane came back for Sam and Mulder for Scully, Buffy finally destroyed Sunnydale in order to save it and Al Giardello's name went up on the board in black. *Who* had added many powerful endings and exits to this list: departures, regenerations, abandonments, marriages, destructions, deaths, escapes. But, as cancellation fell, the Doctor just walked away from Perivale with Ace. A monologue was hastily added over the parting shot. 'There are worlds out there where the sky is burning, where the sea's asleep and the rivers dream, people made of smoke and cities made of song. Somewhere there's danger, somewhere there's injustice and somewhere else the tea is getting cold. Come on, Ace, we've got work to do.' It would feel more final without the last sentence, for – on the cosmic scale of things – it's easier to care about the eternal tea than this year's sidekick. Significantly, this is almost the first time in twenty-eight years that the Doctor has referred to wandering and adventuring as 'work'. Of course, *Doctor Who* had become a chore for everyone, not excluding the audience, and so maybe the last word *should* stand.

5 Survival

Dr Kimble was reincarnated for film and TV remakes (though the real story would have been how a paranoid with a justifiable belief that the authorities were out to get him could ever fit back into society), Terry came back to complicate Bob's later life, *M*A*S*H* veterans found peacetime vocations in *Trapper John, M.D.* (1979) and *After M*A*S*H* (1980), Blake's 7 at least showed up in radio dramas, the Crossroads motel re-opened in the afternoons, Frasier Crane left Boston for his own long-running show, Detective Munch of *Homicide: Life on the Street* (1993–) transferred to *Law & Order: Special Victims Unit* (1999–) just as Spike hopped from *Buffy* (1997–2003) to *Angel* (1999–2004) for another season before that had its own cliffhanger finish. Morse and Meldrew are still dead and the X-Files closed, but it's early days yet. On television, anything which was ever successful is liable to be successful again. Something which lasted as long as *Doctor Who* doesn't evaporate just because one controller of BBC1 can't stand the thought of making any more of it.

In many ways, the 1989 cancellation was not a catastrophe for the *Doctor Who* franchise. Without the focus of an often-embarrassing television show, *Who* lived on as a range of video (then DVD) releases, several lines of books (novelisations of TV scripts and original fiction, an entire library of non-fiction), ongoing periodicals, collections of comic strips, audio dramas ranging from BBC-produced efforts like 'The Paradise of Death' (1993) to outsourced

Surviving on audio

All for charity, Part 1:
'Dimensions in Time' –
even the Cyberman is
grinning!

product like 'The Juggernauts' (2005), video fan fiction like *Downtime* (1995) and *Daemos Rising* (2003), webcast semi-animations like 'Scream of the Shalka' (2003) and 'Real Time' (2004), more merchandising (toys, games, clothing, plates, calendars) than in the early days of 'Dalekmania', conventions and personal appearances, websites,[52] referential strands in TV drama like *G.B.H.* (1991) and *Queer as Folk* (1999), skits on the radio and TV versions on *Dead Ringers* (2002–), charity larks like 'Dimensions in Time' (1993) and 'The Curse of Fatal Death' (1999), the cameo appearance of some 'movie' Daleks in *Looney Tunes Back in Action* (2003), etc. Between 1990 and 2005, it was possible to be a *Doctor Who* fan without ever having watched *Doctor Who*. Among all this activity, it was easy to overlook the revival of the show in a co-production between the BBC and America's Universal intended as a series pilot but eventually just a one-off TV movie.

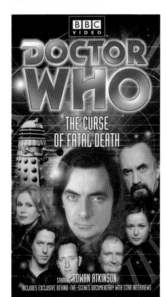

All for charity, Part 2: 'The Curse of Fatal Death'

Doctor Who (1996) is a pendant on the model of 'revival' or 'reunion' TV movies like *The Return of the Man from U.N.C.L.E.* (1983), the *Callan* sequel, *Wet Job* (1981), or *Doomwatch: Winter Angel* (1999). It stands in relationship to the original as various *Star Trek* successors do to *Star Trek* (1966–9) or *The New Avengers* (1976–7) to *The Avengers* (1961–8). This is not necessarily a bad thing – arguably, *Whatever Happened to the Likely Lads?* (1973–4) was a deeper, funnier, more affecting show than *The Likely Lads* (1965–9). If there is a common theme to series revivals it is that time moves on – which is what gives Bob and Terry's slide into young middle age real comic poignance, and tends in the likes of *I Spy Returns* (1994) or the later big-screen *Star Trek* sequels to give rise to jokes about how elderly or frail the once-dashing original cast members have become. The tagline for *Doctor Who* (1996) was 'He's back, and it's about time'. The convention of regeneration theoretically frees the film from middle-aged malaise, but the weight of the show's history and the nature of a Time Lord's life-cycle mean it is even *more* caught up with passing time. Sylvester McCoy is the sole cast hold-over; in the years since 'Survival' (1989) he has lost Ace and gained an interesting, introspective gravitas – short-lived since he is gunned down, then killed on an operating table (by his next incarnation's love interest), but comes back, in a scene intercut with highlights of *Frankenstein* (1931), as a traumatised, hesitant, shrouded Paul McGann.

This Doctor assembles his wardrobe (and personality) exactly as Jon Pertwee does in 'Spearhead from Space' (1970), by stealing clothes from a hospital locker-room, then runs about near-future San Francisco trying to defeat a Master (Eric Roberts) who is after his body,[53] mildly romance a heart specialist (Daphne Ashbrook) and prevent the Earth from being destroyed by a tinkered-with TARDIS. With the production values of mid-range, shot-in-Canada, American television come dumb ideas that overwrite the basics in unhelpful ways. This Doctor had a human mother (like Mr Spock!), these Time Lords have diplomatic relations with Skaro and trust the Dalek legal system (!?) to dispose of the Master, and this TARDIS is powered by the equivalent of a colossally unstable nuclear reactor that can destroy a solar system as a side-effect if a random Earthling puts his or her eye into a beam of light. *Doctor Who* (1963–89) had its own problems, but ran long enough to ignore inconvenient bits of continuity[54] and get on with business. As a one-off, *Doctor Who* (1996) is stuck with half-formed notions of what might work in a transatlantic incarnation of the programme that never eventuated. Despite a poor wig, McGann makes a fair fist of the role. For much of the running time, his Doctor is stuck with the sort of just-regenerated looning Tom Baker does in 'Robot' (1974–5) and Colin Baker in 'The Twin Dilemma' (1984), but when

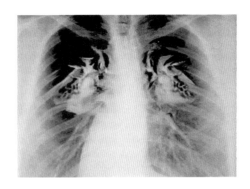

Two hearts, *Doctor Who* (1996)

that is out of the way McGann finds a workable reading. Impulsive, open (if the heart is the centre of feeling, this would explain why McGann has emotion enough for two), eager to share knowledge even if he knows he should keep it to himself, the Eighth Doctor might have been a contender. Then again, problems in pilots tend to be exaggerated rather than solved by subsequent series. The TV movie was gratefully swallowed by the franchise and fandom, and Paul McGann's Doctor slipped into the increasingly convoluted history of the character and the cultural phenomenon.[55]

What *Doctor Who* (1996) *didn't* do was re-establish the Doctor as an ongoing player in mainstream British television. This was left to *Doctor Who* (2005–). Like the TV movie, the new series needs to be seen as separate from the 1963–89 show and plays by different rules.

The Master as action movie villain (Eric Roberts)

Doctor Who (Paul McGann)

With widescreen, film-look visuals (augmented by fairly sophisticated CGI) the series tries not to seem as homemade (ie: cheap) beside current US TV fantasy/science fiction/horror like, say, *Lost* (2004–) or *Battlestar Galactica* (2004–) as *Who* in the 1960s did next to *Star Trek*. Far less 'Americanised' than the TV movie, and indeed given to extended digs at the conventions of US TV, the revival still adopts a structure made familiar by American series in the last two decades: forty-five-minute stand-alone stories, with the occasional two-parter, and soap-like continuing threads and arcs across a season.[56] It even relies on the occasional 'Previously . . .' montage and, on first broadcast, the practice of inserting teaser trailers for next week's episode into the end credits.[57] Perhaps more significant is a subtler change: previous eras within the history of *Doctor Who* (1963–89) were defined by who played the Doctor, with only fan scholars paying attention to the comings and goings of script editors, producers and BBC regimes and the way behind-the-scenes personnel changes shape the programme. *Doctor Who* (2005–) was from the first seen, even outside fan circles, as *authored*. Russell T. Davies, who demonstrated in *Queer as Folk* that he was simultaneously a major television writer and an archetypal *Who* fan-geek, served as script editor and co-producer and wrote a majority of the initial run of episodes. He is as deserving of the 'Created by' credit Alfred Gough and Miles Millar have on *Smallville* (2001–) or the 'Developed for television' credit accorded Deborah Joy LeVine on *Lois*

113

& Clark: The New Adventures of Superman (1993–7).[58] Davies' real achievement with Doctor Who (2005–) is in starting all over again.

Doctor Who (1996), in theory a more radical revision than Doctor Who (2005–), acts as if it were picking up immediately from Doctor Who (1963–89), but Davies' season opener 'Rose' doesn't feel a need to bring on Paul McGann for a regeneration scene.[59] Instead, he takes an approach unused since 'An Unearthly Child' (1963), and starts not with the Doctor in the TARDIS but a viewpoint character, nineteen-year-old Rose Tyler (Billie Piper), who initially has no idea how vast and strange the universe is before she is drawn into the orbit of the charismatic wanderer in time and space. The Autons – last seen in 'Terror of the Autons' (1971) – restage their invasion of London, but what would once have been primary story material is here the B-plot, muddling on in the background and a few effects set-pieces while the real business of the drama is Rose's increasing involvement with the Doctor. The climax is not the destruction of the 'Nestene Consciousness' with a perfunctory anti-plastic MacGuffin but Rose's impulsive decision to accept the Doctor's offer of a berth in the TARDIS; in effect, to sign up for the series. Over the course of thirteen episodes, Davies and the other writers stay surprisingly close to Earth as they deliver variations on classic Who formats: historical/science fictional ('The Unquiet Dead', 'The Empty Child'/'The Doctor Dances'), the invasion of near-contemporary Britain by evil aliens ('Rose', 'Aliens of London'/'World War Three', 'Boom Town'), futuristic space opera ('The End of the World'), dystopian satire ('The Long Game'), famous monsters ('Dalek', 'Bad Wolf'/'The Parting of the Ways') and time-travel paradox ('Father's Day'). The one Who subgenre not tackled is an adventure on a far-off planet, though 'The End of the World' has a mix of exotic, suspicious non-human creatures and murder mystery plotting that harks back to 'The Curse of Peladon' (1972) and 'The Robots of Death' (1977). Often, the business of individual stories (evil extradimensional beings posing as ghosts in 'The Unquiet Dead') is given less weight than continuing strands, chiefly Rose's developing attachment to the Doctor and the toll it takes on her other relationships and the steady drip of revelations about the Time War which has made this Doctor (as things stand) the last Time Lord in the universe.

Though Davies began by clearing the decks, some of the clutter crept back immediately: farting alien jokes, celebrity cameos, DouglasAdamsian silly names ('Blon Fel Fotch Pasameer-Day Slitheen'), over-reliance on the sonic screwdriver (and even the TARDIS) to get out of plot problems and a new sense of précis-like haste to replace the padding of the older serials (there's still a lot of running around, but now it's much *faster*). However, the strength of Davies' approach is its concentration on emotional resonance: a consistent theme is the heroism not just of the Doctor but the people he gets involved with, which even manifests as a hymn to the Blitz spirit ('one damp little island says "no" ') of wartime Britain. A recurrent plot device finds other characters (the maid in 'The Unquiet Dead', Rose's father in 'Father's Day') sacrificing their lives to save humanity or the fabric of the universe. The series finds ways of caring about famous waxworks (Simon Callow as Charles Dickens) or supposed ultimate evil (the nearly redeemed monster of 'Dalek'). Eccleston's caring, committed, slightly smug, slightly sulky, leather-jacketed Ninth Doctor (it is noted that 'U-boat captain' is not a good look for visiting Britain in 1941) is a long way from the Tom Baker who barely noticed the death of a sympathetic character in 'Pyramids of Mars' (1974) but also from the Peter Davison who whines 'there should have been another way' after factions have wiped each other out in 'Warriors of the Deep' (1984). Both the Doctor and Rose form fast attachments to single-episode supporting characters, and ache if (as often happens) they get killed, but there's a darker streak too. In 'The End of the World', the Doctor allows a villain to self-destruct, decreeing that there's a time for everything to die, which he even extends to the planet Earth. An entire episode, 'Boom Town', is somewhat speciously built around a debate between the Doctor and a mass-murdering alien villain (Annette Badland) in which the Time Lord seems to take on board the criticism that he is as prone to wreaking chaos as saving the day. All this might not be the Doctor as he was in the old days, but it is not without precedent. Even the moments of loneliness and despair Eccleston's Doctor shows as a sole survivor might have been picked up from hints here and there in William Hartnell's reading.

While much of Davies' project with the new series has been to polish what always worked about *Doctor Who* and set it going again, the lengthy hiatus since the show was in regular production prompts an amazing number of moments or ideas that, in retrospect, seem so obvious it's a wonder they hadn't been done before: the phone in the TARDIS actually ringing (with that 'for the use of the public' hatch finally opened), the revelation of what those pod-like globules on the lower half of a Dalek do, the Doctor rushing back to the TARDIS during a temporal collapse to find it has turned into a police telephone box, the treatment of the Doctor as an alien abductor by the loved ones of a companion, a full reveal of what the mutant inside a Dalek casing looks like. The series, as ever, engages with its times: casually killing off a Prime Minister who is almost certainly Tony Blair in 'Aliens of London' (his evil replacement attempts to launch a missile strike on the grounds that weapons are circling the Earth which can be deployed in 'forty-five seconds') and creating a surprising number of villains whose schemes

116

Doctor Who (Christopher Eccleston) and Rose (Billie Piper)

boil down to unethical profit-chasing. Does Season One of *Doctor Who* (2005–) set in stone a format which hitherto survived by embracing change? The handover from Ninth to Tenth Doctor seems to be the least traumatic recasting of the series' lead in its history, with the regeneration of Christopher Eccleston into David Tennant apparently built into the overall story from the first. Having been away so long and striven so hard to be fresh on its return – even Michael Grade noticed – *Who* might in 2005 be under pressure to stay the same for a while, even with a fresh face in the lead, in order not to alienate the new audience the programme has found. However, this near-casual regeneration may also be down to the fact that Davies' particular take on the format revolves not around the Doctor, whom he inherited, but *Rose*, whom he created (she's written much better than the superficially similar Ace was in the 1980s). In 'The Parting of the Ways', Rose briefly became more powerful than any entity previously encountered in time and space, which solved one set of problems (the renascent Daleks) but also prompted the regeneration (triggered by a kiss, which in itself sets another precedent); the next real shake-up for the show might come when Billie Piper leaves the cast, no matter who is the Doctor at that time.

117

Doctor Who survived for so long, and will return in forms known and unknown, thanks to processes inherent in the premise even before someone hit on the notion that the Doctor could regenerate. At the end, we return to the beginning, and the blue box. 'Bigger on the inside than the outside' is already a paradox, set aside by a transdimensional thinking which embeds an inconsistency and makes what should be a flaw[60] an opportunity for limitless adventure. 'TARDIS' and 'Dalek' have made the *Oxford English Dictionary*, and 'Time Lord' probably ought to, but the most insidious *Who* coinage, rarely noticed, is the delightfully suggestive 'dematerialisation circuit'. This is the component of a time machine that packs everything up after each trip and removes it from the material world, a process presumably reversed by a never-mentioned 'materialisation circuit' to begin the cycle anew. By comparison, the *Star Trek* transporter is mundane pseudo-

Rose (Billie Piper) and Doctor Who (David Tennant)

science, reducing people to constituent atoms and transmitting
('beaming') them to a new location. *Dematerialisation* is more radical
than deconstruction, a violation of the law that forms can be changed
but not destroyed, let alone the common-sense principle that once
something has ceased to exist it can't be conjured up again in real life.
It's a process repeated time and time again, with that classic wheezing
sound effect and the rise and fall of the TARDIS console, and an *idea* so
thrilling, complex and vast that quantum physicists, let alone TV
creators and viewers, could go mad if they pondered it for more than
twenty-five minutes at a stretch.

  The TARDIS, and everyone in it, dematerialised at the end of
'An Unearthly Child', forfeiting any place they might have had in the
normal world inside and outside a television set. Since then, they have
been *somewhere else*.

Notes

1 During the 1969–70 hiatus, *Star Trek*'s first British run was scheduled in the *Doctor Who* Saturday slot. When it seemed the future of *Who* might be in doubt and fans wrote to the BBC's *Junior Points of View* feedback programme, host Robert Robinson introduced a clip from the *Star Trek* episode 'Arena' – the first UK glimpse of the already-cancelled series – to assure young science-fiction devotees that they would not be neglected.

2 At the time of writing, the institution is again open for business. Scheduled at 7.00 on Saturday evenings, between *Strictly Come Dancing* (2004–) and the *National Lottery* (1998–), the 2005 reformatting has – somewhat surprisingly, but pleasingly – exceeded expectations of a nostalgia gimmick along the lines of the Vic Reeves–Bob Mortimer take on *Randall and Hopkirk (Deceased)* (2000–1) and been embraced by an audience broad enough to disqualify the show from the 'cult' label.

3 A TV programme is said to have 'jumped the shark' when it has passed the peak of creativity or popular acceptance and declined into a feeble imitation of itself. The term derives from an episode of *Happy Days* (1974–84) in which the Fonz performs a waterskiing stunt involving dangerous fish. Other typical 'jump the shark' moments include the introduction of Scrappy-Doo in *Scooby and Scrappy-Doo*

(1979–83, the second reformatting of *Scooby-Doo, Where Are You?*, 1969–73) or David and Maddie actually sleeping together on *Moonlighting* (1985–9).

4 At first, *Doctor Who* serials had overall titles *and* individual episode titles; eg: 'The Aztecs' consists of 'The Temple of Death', 'The Warriors of Death', 'The Bride of Sacrifice' and 'The Day of Darkness'. At the outset, the overall serial titles tended to be used only in-house and variants exist: '100,000 BC' is also known as 'The Tribe of Gum', while controversy persists over whether the second serial should be called 'The Daleks' or 'The Mutants' (which raises confusion, since there's a 1972 serial of the same name). Occasionally, there was an overlap: for instance, Episode One of 'The Space Museum' is called 'The Space Museum'. Video and DVD releases tend to use the serial titles, though '100,000 BC' is usually seen under the title of its first, near stand-alone episode, 'An Unearthly Child'. From 'The Savages' (1966) on, the individual episode titles were dropped.

5 Presumably, this serves as a declaration of intent, 'I am for man'. The Doctor has certainly been in favour of the human race. Given the general tone taken with Earthlings early on, it could be 'I am 'fore man' in the sense of being more advanced than humanity. Or 'foreman', in the sense of being in charge of the shop floor. Until 1980, it could have been construed as 'I

am four-man'. It could, of course, just be a name.

6 The thin man of *The Thin Man* (1934) isn't Nick Charles, but the victim of the murder he solves; this was remembered as the first few sequels – *After the Thin Man* (1936) and *Another Thin Man* (1939) – scrupulously referred to the case rather than the detective, but the situation changed with *The Thin Man Goes Home* (1944) where, by going home, Nick explicitly becomes the Thin Man of the title. The Rockford files are at police headquarters: the original premise of *The Rockford Files* (1974–80) was that Jim (James Garner) only worked 'unsolved or inactive' police cases. The actual cabinets are seen under the titles of the pilot; when the series came along the 'cold cases' angle was too limiting and so the files were rarely visited.

7 In 'Logopolis', the gadget is renamed a 'chameleon circuit'. *Doctor Who* (1996) controversially uses the term 'cloaking device' – poached from *Star Trek*.

8 Note to Americans or those born after 1965. Before the 1970s, British children sat an exam at the age of eleven, at the end of their years at primary school (grade school). If they passed, they would go on to a grammar school; if they failed, they would go on to a secondary modern school. On the whole, the system was replaced in the 1970s by comprehensive schools – though some grammar schools persist. Middle-class parents who lament the extinction of grammars rarely agitate for the return of secondary moderns for kids labelled as failures at the age of eleven.

9 This instrument is established earlier, as the Doctor checks the radiation levels on prehistoric Earth before venturing out. Then, it is practically forgotten as serials got away from the radioactive obsessions almost inevitable in science fiction in the early 1960s.

10 The Doctor would not get proper love interest until regenerated into the young and presentable Paul McGann for *Doctor Who* (1996). He was *apparently* asexual again by 'Rose' (2005), where he deftly dodges a pass from Rose's mother (Camille Coduri). Throughout *Doctor Who* (2005–), Rose (Billie Piper) keeps denying that she and the Doctor are a couple – though her potential love interests tend to be dysfunctionally feckless fellows with 'Sell by End of Season' stamped on their foreheads. It's clear that *something* complicated is going on between the girl and her alien mentor – they are both jealous of any possible replacements who might float in and out of the plot. The twenty-first century incarnation of the programme tends to point up any subtexts about attractions among the TARDIS crew, even if they are impossible to act on. The bisexual Jack Harkness (John Barrowman), whom Rose fancies, has a slight crush on the Ninth Doctor.

11 'Barbara Wright' seems to have been named for her knack of making 'right' guesses. Of course, as a teacher, she is also 'Miss Right'.

12 Davros owes something to another big-domed, stunted, chair-assisted master villain, the Mekon – arch-enemy of the *Eagle* comic's space-faring hero Dan Dare. Frank Hampson's 1950 introductory Dan Dare serial, 'Pilot of the Future' (usually reprinted as 'Voyage to Venus') features a Dalek–Thal-like race conflict on Venus, between the aggressive, militarist, green-skinned, scientific Treens and the long-haired, blond, humanist, pacifist Therons.

13 Paul Cornell reminds me it was Kit-Kat. The clients must be delighted to have funded such an expensive, all-star ad campaign – besides the Daleks, it featured a host of other semi-famous faces from Motörhead's Lemmy to Lawrence Llewellyn-Bowen – which I could recall in every single detail except for the pack shot at the end, or even the variety of item being hawked. Holding up a cardboard sign reading 'eat Kit-Kat' would have been more effective.

14 See, for instance, *Doctor Who: The Handbook: The Second Doctor: The Patrick Troughton Years: 1966–1969* (Virgin, 1997) by David J. Howe, Mark Stammers and Stephen James Walker, and *Doctor Who: The Sixties* (Doctor Who/Virgin, 1992) by the same authors.

15 I owned a plastic Mechanoid, representative of a robot race who had a war with the Daleks – but only ever appeared in *two episodes* of 'The Chase' (1965). The existence of the toy suggests the BBC's still-amateur merchandising department, baffled but pleased by the enormous success of Dalek tie-ins, thought there might be another bonanza in these croaking, bloated loser Dalek rip-offs. The Mechanoids missed so widely that they didn't even return in the mid-1980s, when *Doctor Who* was dredging its backlist for enemies who might do for another serial or two.

16 Similar effects were achieved, to slightly more sacrilegious ends, by Michael Moorcock in 'Behold the Man' (1966) and George R. R. Martin in the *Twilight Zone* episode 'The Once and Future King' (1986). In these tales, circumstances force time travellers to replace disappointing real people and live out the legends of Jesus Christ and Elvis Presley. Moorcock probably saw 'The Myth Makers' around the time he was writing his award-winning story.

17 Not to mention slash fiction possibilities between the 80s Doctor and sulky schoolboys Adric and Turlough.

18 This is a rare and welcome instance of other characters even noticing how odd the regulars look. No 1980s guest character ever mentions that Nicola Bryant's Peri is dressed like a porn star, though even giant earthworms and barbarian chiefs express an interest in having sex with her. A typical Peri line is a shuddered 'dirty old warlord'.

19 Romance between old folks would, of course, be a major switch-off for the show's perceived demographic if 'The Aztecs' were in development now.

20 Langford, who lasted exactly as long as the aptly named Dodo, is the only *Doctor Who* companion generally remembered by the name of the performer rather than the character (who was called Mel). This is a perilous strategy for a fragile ego. Whereas viewers reacted against the annoying *character* of Adric rather than Matthew Waterhouse's performance, Bonnie Langford took all the blame. The highlight of her run is in 'Time and the Rani' (1987), when the Rani (Kate O'Mara) does a funny Langford impersonation to mess with the scrambled mind of the just-regenerated Sylvester McCoy. Objectively, Mel isn't written or played much worse than the companions who came before or after her.

21 Rowan Atkinson, Richard E. Grant, Jim Broadbent, Hugh Grant and Joanna Lumley – all surprisingly decent in the role despite a feeble script. Richard E. Grant later played it slightly straighter in the mildly canonical 'In-betweenth Doctor' web-based cartoon 'Scream of the Shalka' (2003).

22 This bit of continuity is filled in during 'The Time Warrior' (1973–4), where the planet of the Time Lords is finally identified as Gallifrey.

23 'Boom Town' (2005) provides a funny explanation for the Doctor's tendency to return to the Earth – you can't get fresh milk anywhere else in the universe.

121

24 In *Doctor Who* (2005–), the Ninth Doctor (Christopher Eccleston) sometimes claims to have been travelling in the TARDIS for 900 years, suggesting a possible 870-odd years-worth of 'missing adventures' since the Eight Doctor (Paul McGann) left Earth at the end of *Doctor Who* (1996). Then again, there could be a gap of centuries somewhere else in the saga, given the varying ages different Doctors have claimed to be.

25 Jamie comes into and leaves *Doctor Who* in serials which make reference to the BBC-TV work of Peter Watkins: 'The Highlanders' (1966–7) to *Culloden* (1964) and 'The War Games' (1969) in title at least to *The War Game* (1965).

26 Ironically, 'The Invasion', set in a very near future almost indistinguishable from 1968, takes place *before* the earlier Cyber-serials, which have more futuristic or outer-space backdrops. Nevertheless, it was in this serial that the Cybermen evolved the large pie-plate 'ears' they would more or less stick with for one-off appearances opposite every Doctor between Tom Baker and Sylvester McCoy.

27 Nicholas Courtney had also been in 'The Daleks' Master Plan', as security agent Bret Vyon.

28 *Doctor Who* had bridged a seven-week gap in the summer of 1968, between its fifth and sixth seasons, with a repeat of 'The Evil of the Daleks' (1967). Uniquely, this was inserted into the continuity of the show by having the Doctor project mental experiences of a past adventure to warn Zoe of the sort of perils she's liable to face if she joins the crew of the TARDIS. This was also the only serial to be repeated in its entirety in the 1960s.

29 The filtering of these authors' material through *Doctor Who* would shape adaptations of their own work. BBC-TV

dramatisations of *The Day of the Triffids* (1981) and *The Invisible Man* (1984), from former *Who* producers (David Maloney, Barry Letts), use the twenty-five-minute episode serial-with-a-cliffhanger format and have much of the look and feel of *Who*. Innes Lloyd, an earlier producer on the show, was responsible for Nigel Kneale's masterly ghost story *The Stone Tape* (1973) and the overlooked invasion-themed Nazis-won-the-war serial *An Englishman's Castle* (1978).

30 Arthur C. Clarke put this idea forward in *Childhood's End* (1954), well before Kneale's serial.

31 *Invasion* is based on a story by Robert Holmes and *Night of the Big Heat* was co-scripted by Pip and Jane Baker, all frequent *Doctor Who* writers.

32 Though the *Star Trek* episode 'Mirror, Mirror' (1967) – the one which visits the universe where Spock has a beard and Kirk gained captaincy of the *Enterprise* by assassinating Christopher Pike – predates 'Inferno', the parallel reality concept was not yet a commonplace. Now, all shows are obliged to do at least one alternative timeline episode (eg: 'The Wish', *Buffy the Vampire Slayer*, 1998; 'Netherworld', *The Dead Zone*, 2002). *Sliders* (1994–2000) consists of nothing but jumps into other Earths and *Six Feet Under* (2001–) opened its third season with 'Perfect Circles' in which, either in anaesthetised fantasy or through genuine time-tripping, protagonist Nate Fisher visits a bewildering number of alternative timelines. Considering the potential of the form and *Doctor Who*'s need for material, it's surprising that the show didn't venture sideways in time again – though Dalek stories from 'Genesis of the Daleks' (1975) to 'Remembrance of the Daleks' (1988) take place on a timeline altered from that laid down by serials from

122

'The Daleks' (1963–4) to 'Death to the Daleks' (1974). And 'Battlefield' (1989) features visitors from a sword-and-sorcery continuum.

33 When writer Ian McDonald was called in to pitch ideas for what became the revival TV movie, *Doomwatch: Winter Angel* (1999), he ran through a list of cutting-edge millennial hot topics only to discover the 1970–3 show had with remarkable foresight covered them all.

34 Nigel Kneale's TV adaptation of *Nineteen Eighty-Four* (1954) and his original play *The Year of the Sex Olympics* (1968) set precedents for satirical science fiction on television, and also came up with conventions of art direction and costuming that *Doctor Who* would follow in its depiction of various futuristic societies. Less well remembered is *The Adventures of Don Quick* (1970), with Ian Hendry and Ronald Lacey as spacefaring equivalents of Don Quixote and Sancho Panza, which was almost an anti-*Who*. Like the Doctor, Don often shows up on a planet where society has evolved in a freakish direction and proceeds to shake things up – but he always pushes the worlds he visits into disasters, departing blithely certain of his benevolence before the worst happens. 'The Higher, the Fewer' prefigures *Who*'s 'Paradise Towers' (1988) in depicting a stratified civilisation that lives entirely inside a tower block.

35 Any reputation the show had for accurate prediction of political events, based on the moment where the Brigadier addresses the PM as 'madam' over the telephone in 'Terror of the Zygons', should be balanced by noting that in 'The Green Death' (1973) the PM is called 'Jeremy' – suggesting the later 1970s should have seen Liberal Jeremy Thorpe as Prime Minister rather than retired in disgrace after a homosexual scandal.

36 For instance, how could they miss having a cliffhanger with the current Doctor regenerating as the Valeyard, then spending some episodes cheerfully murdering the Doctor's companions as Angel (David Boreanaz) did when temporarily returned to his evil vampire form Angelus on *Buffy the Vampire Slayer* (1997–2003)?

37 Sally Pike, who was in Geography with me in 1974–5, said the robot in 'Robot' was the first *Doctor Who* monster *not* to scare her. Since this must have included the notoriously feeble Kronos of 'The Time Monster' (1972), it remains a damning statement.

38 For instance, we have never found out who Susan's parents were. Or, of course, whether the Doctor has a name. After four decades, these mysteries should perhaps remain unexplored. Imposed solutions tend to muddy rather than clarify the issue, as with the revelation of the Doctor's hitherto-unsuspected half-human nature in *Doctor Who* (1996).

39 There was also another shift in the scheduling, moving towards an American programming pattern. *Doctor Who* no longer commenced its annual new series in the BBC's 'Week One' (the first episode of 'Robot' was transmitted on 28 December 1974, whereas Pertwee seasons always began in early January). For the rest of the 1970s, the programme returned at the end of the summer, usually in the back-to-school month of September, and ran until March or April.

40 *Doctor Who* would not get round to *proper* alien vampires until 'State of Decay' (1980), though a robot Dracula had popped up in 'The Chase' (1966). By contrast, *Star Trek* did its 'salt vampire' story for its first regularly screened episode, 'The Man Trap' (1966).

41 Baker starred in *The Hound of the*

123

124

Baskervilles (1982), a 'BBC Classic Serial' produced by *Who* veteran Barry Letts.

42 When the Doctor appeared on *The Simpsons* ('Sideshow Bob's Last Gleaming', 1995), it was in the likeness of Tom Baker.

43 The break-out star and backbone of *Doctor Who* (2005–) was not Christopher Eccleston, admirable though he might be, but Billie Piper – whom many feared would be the twenty-first century answer to Bonnie Langford. Piper's Rose turned out to be such a strong presence that, in a development which skews the premise in a manner which will be difficult to follow up, the Season One closer 'Bad Wolf'/'The Parting of the Ways' positions her (temporarily) as a cosmically powered being on a scale with Marvel Comics' Silver Surfer or Dark Phoenix.

44 A strike at ITV in 1979 certainly helped.

45 1980s ratings fail to take into account the new, significant audience segment who videotaped the programme to watch later. Many of *Doctor Who*'s most devoted fans fell into this category, establishing their own libraries on cassette well before official retail releases of the *Who* backlist. Earlier fans had *audio*-taped serials – these are now the only surviving versions of much 1960s *Who*. Viewing figures for the series can be found in *The Television Companion: The Unofficial and Unauthorised Guide to* Doctor Who by David J. Howe and Stephen James Walker.

46 Though posters at <www.jumptheshark. com> tend to disagree. Many cite the arrival of Peter Davison or Colin Baker as the point of no return.

47 Just like five-year-olds of 1999 allegedly loved Jar-Jar Binks.

48 In Doctor Who*: The Discontinuity Guide* (1995), Paul Cornell, Martin Day and Keith Topping point out that the opening shots of the Rudolph Cartier-directed *Nineteen Eighty-Four* and 'The Sun Makers' are identical.

49 'The Five Doctors' is arguably the first *Doctor Who* TV movie, though occasional serials ('Genesis of the Daleks', for instance) were edited into feature-length omnibus shows in the 1970s. The first BBC video releases tended to trim individual episode titles and splice together cliffhangers and escapes, before purists insisted they be issued as originally broadcast. Following the pattern of UK Gold's cruder edited omnibus broadcasts, most modern viewers on DVD or video tend to watch the serials *as if they were* features, fast-forwarding through end titles and recaps. Some stories play much better taken in twenty-five-minute bites with a week of suspense between each episode.

50 Paul Cornell, who strongly disagrees with this statement, reminds me that Nicholas Parsons – in theory the lightweight of this crowd – gives the best dramatic performance, in the often-impressive but typically incoherent 'The Curse of Fenric' (1989).

51 In *Chikyu Boeigun* (*The Mysterians*, 1957), Japan is invaded by ethnically oriental extra-terrestrials who speak Japanese, albeit in that halting, learned-from-your-radio-broadcasts manner popular with all manner of aliens.

52 Start with <www.bbc.co.uk/cult/ doctorwho/links.shtml>, which is the BBC's official site, but then check out <www.gallifreyone.net>, an impressive fan site, and for a more exhausting distraction from whatever you were trying to look up in the first place, go to <www.doctorwhoweb guide.net>.

53 British *Doctor Who*, especially in the 1980s, was not free of camp, but it took an American co-production to do a full-on action movie homoerotic crackle between macho enemies, complete with McGann in a bondage scene and Roberts spurning the come-on of a human woman who thinks he's her husband in order to obsess about getting into the Doctor's body. That the process of Time Lord possession is highly sexualised is demonstrated when the Master takes on the human form of 'Bruce', a paramedic played by Roberts – an ectoplasmic snake-phallus enters Bruce orally and leaves him looking like the startled recipient of a messy facial cum shot.

54 As with the Sherlock Holmes stories, a fannish industry has arisen to address the problems of 'continuity', elaborately rationalising away impossible dates, irreconcilable statements, downright mistakes and we-just-plain-don't-care-and-want-to-get-on-with-the-story contrivances. Along with this come arguments as to whether books, comics, unproduced scripts or certain TV stories liked less than others count as part of the canon and should be acknowledged as such. It strikes me as curmudgeonly to criticise Sir Arthur Conan Doyle for making 'errors', like having Mrs Watson get her husband's first name wrong on one occasion or giving Moriarty the same first name as his brother. He was writing before there was much tradition of consistency in series fiction, when writers and readers tended not to care that a specific date in 1889 represented as a Wednesday in fiction was a Saturday on the calendar. Furthermore, there's a certain lack of gratitude to the actual author of the stories in the mock-serious insistence that Doyle was merely Dr Watson's 'literary agent', responsible for getting dates 'wrong' or covering up the 'real' nature of Watson's war-wound. As the creator of Sherlock Holmes and his world, Doyle was entitled to write whatever he wanted, contradict

himself if he felt like it or make things up on the spur of the moment; if that wasn't good enough for generations of readers, then there wouldn't be a Holmes fandom or 'higher criticism' in the first place. Similarly, *Who* nit-picking boils down to a wish that the show was not a continually rewritten fiction but a body of obscured truth, to be treated like the *original* canon (the writings which make up the Bible) and sifted through for a definitive version (in which the world was created on a particular day in 2004 BC) while all else is relegated to the Apocrypher or cast out as blasphemous. The Holmes stories were written by one man, though pasticheurs have been legion; *Doctor Who* wasn't even *created* by one man in the sense some TV shows acknowledge individual producer–writers as creators – let alone written, directed, enacted, interpreted, costumed or coiffed by a single guiding intelligence. Long-running TV programmes escape their creators and become auteurless constructs, open to random quests for meanings intended and/or fortuitous. Actually, that's quite an interesting enough endeavour *without* having to worry whether William Hartnell's Doctor has two hearts – I'm being petty, here: in my novella 'Time and Relative' (2001), I went with the assumption that all Time Lords are two-hearted, not knowing that some spin-off novels had decided that the Doctor only grew another heart on his first (or second) regeneration – or how the human race manages to forget successive large-scale alien invasions and be surprised by the next one. In 'Remembrance of the Daleks' (1988), Ace claims that if Daleks had invaded Earth in 1963, she would have heard of it, and the Doctor responds 'Do you remember the Zygon gambit with the Loch Ness Monster? Or the Yeti in the Underground? Your species has an amazing

125

capacity for self-deception.' Then the matter quite properly is dropped and they get on with the story. A subtler problem is raised by the same story – it is reasonable to expect that 1988 *viewers* might not remember long-unseen monsters like the Zygons or the Yeti, but they knew who the Daleks were. Ace, apparently, lives in a universe where there is a Doctor but no *Doctor Who* – though this story, set in the year the show debuted, has a joke about a television being switched off just before 'an adventure in the new science-fiction series *Do-*'. A similar temporal displacement occurs in *Godzilla* (1998), which takes place in a universe where there is (sort of) a Godzilla but there have never been any Godzilla *movies*. Contemporary-set vampire films from *Blacula* (1972) to *Blade Trinity* (2004) have to acknowledge the existence of Dracula as a figure who displaces some cultural water even if they bring on their version of a *real* Dracula.

55 The Eighth Doctor rated a comic strip in the *Radio Times* and more 'further adventures' novels than other, more established incarnations. McGann reprised the role on audio, most accessibly in a webcast production of 'Shada', a Douglas Adams script abandoned in mid-production in 1980 due to industrial action (a version was released on BBC video in 1992). Though mounted in homage to the late Adams, who had already cannibalised his scripts in his *Dirk Gently* books, 'Shada' was rewritten by other hands to fit into 'continuity', dragging the Eighth Doctor back in time to team with Romana (Lalla Ward) and K9.

56 The last gasp of the original format, twenty-five-minute episodes mostly or entirely shot-on-video-look video, was writer Neil Gaiman's interesting but not terribly successful fantasy serial, *Neverwhere* (1996).

57 This device is problematic when used after a cliffhanger, of course. Another problem emerged over the course of the 2005 season as even fine episodes found it hard to compete with expectations raised by brilliantly cut-together trailers.

58 The point being that *Smallville* and *Lois & Clark* are both based on characters created by Jerome Siegel and Joe Shuster and developed by many other hands since 1938, but make their own distinct, critically (indeed legally) definable uses of the world of Superman.

59 Though Christopher Eccleston quickly established his own take on the role, Paul McGann could quite easily have played the 2005 Doctor.

60 Imagine how fan scholars would cope if Conan Doyle had established that 221B had more windows onto Baker Street than could be observed from outside the rooms.

Credits

Doctor Who

Production Company: British
Broadcasting Corporation ©
BBC Worldwide

Series One
Regular Cast
William Hartnell (The Doctor)
William Russell (Ian
Chesterton)
Jacqueline Hill (Barbara
Wright)
Carole Ann Ford (Susan
Foreman)
Pilot episode
(unaired until 26/08/1991)
100,000 BC (four parts)
23/11/1963 An Unearthly
Child
30/11/1963 The Cave of Skulls
7/12/1963 The Forest of Fear
14/12/1963 The Firemaker
The Daleks (seven parts)
21/12/1963 The Dead Planet
28/12/1963 The Survivors
4/1/1964 The Escape
11/1/1964 The Ambush
18/1/1964 The Expedition
25/1/1964 The Ordeal
1/2/1964 The Rescue
The Edge of Destruction aka
Inside the Spaceship (two
parts)
8/2/1964 The Edge of
Destruction
15/2/1964 The Brink of Disaster
Marco Polo (seven parts)
22/2/1964 The Roof of the
World
29/2/1964 The Singing
Sands
7/3/1964 Five Hundred Eyes
14/3/1964 The Wall of Lies
21/3/1964 Rider from Shang-Tu
28/3/1964 Mighty Kublai
Khan
4/4/1964 Assassin at Peking
The Keys of Marinus (six parts)

11/4/1964 The Sea of Death
18/4/1964 The Velvet Web
25/4/1964 The Screaming
Jungle
2/5/1964 The Snows of Terror
9/5/1964 Sentence of Death
16/5/1964 The Keys of
Marinus
The Aztecs (four parts)
23/5/1964 The Temple of
Evil
30/5/1964 The Warriors of
Death
6/6/1964 The Bride of
Sacrifice
13/6/1964 The Day of
Darkness
The Sensorites (six parts)
20/6/1964 Strangers in Space
27/6/1964 The Unwilling
Warriors
11/7/1964 Hidden Danger
18/7/1964 A Race against
Death
25/7/1964 Kidnap
1/8/1964 A Desperate
Venture
The Reign of Terror (six parts)
8/8/1964 A Land of Fear
15/8/1964 Guests of
Madame Guillotine
22/8/1964 A Change of
Identity
29/8/1964 The Tyrant of
France
5/9/1964 A Bargain of
Necessity
12/9/1964 Prisoners of
Conciergerie

Series Two
Regular Cast
William Hartnell (The Doctor)
William Russell (Ian
Chesterton)
Jacqueline Hill (Barbara
Wright)
Carole Ann Ford (Susan
Foreman)

Maureen O'Brien (Vicki)
Peter Purves (Steven Taylor)
Planet of Giants (three parts)
31/10/1964 Planet of Giants
7/11/1964 Dangerous
Journey
14/11/1964 Crisis
The Dalek Invasion of Earth
(six parts)
21/11/1964 World's End
28/11/1964 The Daleks
5/12/1964 Day of Reckoning
12/12/1964 The End of
Tomorrow
19/12/1964 The Waking Ally
26/12/1964 Flashpoint
The Rescue (two parts)
2/1/1965 The Powerful
Enemy
9/1/1965 Desperate
Measures
The Romans (four parts)
16/1/1965 The Slave Traders
23/1/1965 All Roads Lead to
Rome
30/1/1965 Conspiracy
6/2/1965 Inferno
The Web Planet (six parts)
13/2/1965 The Web Planet
20/2/1965 The Zarbi
27/2/1965 Escape to Danger
6/3/1965 Crater of Needles
13/3/1965 Invasion
20/3/1965 The Centre
The Crusade (four parts)
27/3/1965 The Lion
3/4/1965 The Knight of Jaffa
10/4/1965 The Wheel of
Fortune
17/4/1965 The Warlords
The Space Museum (four
parts)
24/4/1965 The Space
Museum
1/5/1965 The Dimensions of
Time
8/5/1965 The Search
15/5/1965 The Final Phase

127

The Chase (six parts)
22/5/1965 The Executioners
29/5/1965 The Death of Time
5/6/1965 Flight through
Eternity
12/6/1965 Journey into
Terror
19/6/1965 The Death of
Doctor Who
26/6/1965 The Planet of
Decision
The Time Meddler (four parts)
3/7/1965 The Watcher
10/7/1965 The Meddling
Monk
17/7/1965 A Battle of Wits
24/7/1965 Checkmate

Series Three
Regular Cast
William Hartnell (The Doctor)
Maureen O'Brien (Vicki)
Peter Purves (Steven Taylor)
Adrienne Hill (Katarina)
Jackie Lane (Dodo Chaplet)
Galaxy 4 (four parts)
11/9/1965 Four Hundred
Dawns
18/9/1965 Trap of Steel
25/9/1965 Air Lock
2/10/1965 The Exploding
Planet
Mission to the Unknown (one
part)
9/10/1965 Mission to the
Unknown
The Myth Makers (four parts)
16/10/1965 Temple of
Secrets
23/10/1965 Small Prophet,
Quick Return
30/10/1965 Death of a Spy
6/11/1965 Horse of
Destruction
The Daleks' Master Plan
(twelve parts)
13/11/1965 The Nightmare
Begins
20/11/1965 Day of
Armageddon
27/11/1965 Devil's Planet
4/12/1965 The Traitors
11/12/1965 Counter Plot
18/12/1965 Coronas of the
Sun

25/12/1965 The Feast of
Steven
1/1/1966 Volcano
8/1/1966 Golden Death
15/1/1966 Escape Switch
22/1/1966 The Abandoned
Planet
29/1/1966 Destruction of
Time
The Massacre aka *The
Massacre of St Bartholomew's
Eve* (four parts)
5/2/1966 War of God
12/2/1966 The Sea Beggar
19/2/1966 Priest of Death
26/2/1966 Bell of Doom
The Ark (four parts)
5/3/1966 The Steel Sky
12/3/1966 The Plague
19/3/1966 The Return
26/3/1966 The Bomb
The Celestial Toymaker (four
parts)
2/4/1966 The Celestial
Toyroom
9/4/1966 The Hall of Dolls
16/4/1966 The Dancing Floor
23/4/1966 The Final Test
The Gunfighters (four parts)
30/4/1966 A Holiday for the
Doctor
7/5/1966 Don't Shoot the
Pianist
14/5/1966 Johnny Ringo
21/5/1966 The O.K. Corral
The Savages (four parts)
28/5/1966 Part One
4/6/1966 Part Two
11/6/1966 Part Three
18/6/1966 Part Four
The War Machines (four parts)
25/6/1966 Part One
2/7/1966 Part Two
9/7/1966 Part Three
16/7/1966 Part Four

Series Four
Regular Cast
William Hartnell/Patrick
Troughton (The Doctor)
Anneke Wills (Polly)
Michael Craze (Ben Jackson)
Frazer Hines (Jamie)
The Smugglers (four parts)
10/9/1966 Part One

17/9/1966 Part Two
24/9/1966 Part Three
1/10/1966 Part Four
The Tenth Planet (four parts)
8/10/1966 Part One
15/10/1966 Part Two
22/10/1966 Part Three
29/10/1966 Part Four
The Power of the Daleks (six
parts)
5/11/1966 Part One
12/11/1966 Part Two
19/11/1966 Part Three
26/11/1966 Part Four
3/12/1966 Part Five
10/12/1966 Part Six
The Highlanders (four parts)
17/12/1966 Part One
24/12/1966 Part Two
31/12/1966 Part Three
7/1/1967 Part Four
The Underwater Menace (four
parts)
14/1/1967 Part One
21/1/1967 Part Two
28/1/1967 Part Three
4/2/1967 Part Four
The Moonbase (four parts)
11/2/1967 Part One
18/2/1967 Part Two
25/2/1967 Part Three
4/3/1967 Part Four
The Macra Terror (four parts)
11/3/1967 Part One
18/3/1967 Part Two
25/3/1967 Part Three
1/4/1967 Part Four
The Faceless Ones (six parts)
8/4/1967 Part One
15/4/1967 Part Two
22/4/1967 Part Three
29/4/1967 Part Four
6/5/1967 Part Five
13/5/1967 Part Six
The Evil of the Daleks (seven
parts)
20/5/1967 Part One
27/5/1967 Part Two
3/6/1967 Part Three
10/6/1967 Part Four
17/6/1967 Part Five
24/6/1967 Part Six
1/7/1967 Part Seven

Series Five
Regular Cast
Patrick Troughton (The Doctor)
Frazer Hines (Jamie)
Deborah Watling (Victoria)
Wendy Padbury (Zoe)
The Tomb of the Cybermen (four parts)
2/9/1967 Part One
9/9/1967 Part Two
16/9/1967 Part Three
23/9/1967 Part Four
The Abominable Snowmen (six parts)
30/9/1967 Part One
7/10/1967 Part Two
14/10/1967 Part Three
21/10/1967 Part Four
28/10/1967 Part Five
4/11/1967 Part Six
The Ice Warriors (six parts)
11/11/1967 Part One
18/11/1967 Part Two
25/11/1967 Part Three
2/12/1967 Part Four
9/12/1967 Part Five
16/12/1967 Part Six
The Enemy of the World (six parts)
23/12/1967 Part One
30/12/1967 Part Two
6/1/1968 Part Three
13/1/1968 Part Four
20/1/1968 Part Five
27/1/1968 Part Six
The Web of Fear (six parts)
3/2/1968 Part One
10/2/1968 Part Two
17/2/1968 Part Three
24/2/1968 Part Four
2/3/1968 Part Five
9/3/1968 Part Six
Fury from the Deep (six parts)
16/3/1968 Part One
23/3/1968 Part Two
30/3/1968 Part Three
6/4/1968 Part Four
13/4/1968 Part Five
20/4/1968 Part Six
The Wheel in Space (six parts)
27/4/1968 Part One
4/5/1968 Part Two
11/5/1968 Part Three

18/5/1968 Part Four
25/5/1968 Part Five
1/6/1968 Part Six

Series Six
Regular Cast
Patrick Troughton (The Doctor)
Frazer Hines (Jamie)
Wendy Padbury (Zoe)
The Dominators (five parts)
10/8/1968 Part One
17/8/1968 Part Two
24/8/1968 Part Three
31/8/1968 Part Four
7/9/1968 Part Five
The Mind Robber (five parts)
14/9/1968 Part One
21/9/1968 Part Two
28/9/1968 Part Three
5/10/1968 Part Four
12/10/1968 Part Five
The Invasion (eight parts)
2/11/1968 Part One
9/11/1968 Part Two
16/11/1968 Part Three
23/11/1968 Part Four
30/11/1968 Part Five
7/12/1968 Part Six
14/12/1968 Part Seven
21/12/1968 Part Eight
The Krotons (four parts)
28/12/1968 Part One
4/1/1969 Part Two
11/1/1969 Part Three
18/1/1969 Part Four
The Seeds of Death (six parts)
25/1/1969 Part One
1/2/1969 Part Two
8/2/1969 Part Three
15/2/1969 Part Four
22/2/1969 Part Five
1/3/1969 Part Six
The Space Pirates (six parts)
8/3/1969 Part One
15/3/1969 Part Two
22/3/1969 Part Three
29/3/1969 Part Four
5/4/1969 Part Five
12/4/1969 Part Six
The War Games (ten parts)
19/4/1969 Part One
26/4/1969 Part Two
3/5/1969 Part Three
10/5/1969 Part Four

17/5/1969 Part Five
24/5/1969 Part Six
31/5/1969 Part Seven
7/6/1969 Part Eight
14/6/1969 Part Nine
21/06/1969 Part Ten

Series Seven
Regular Cast
Jon Pertwee (The Doctor)
Caroline John (Liz Shaw)
Nicholas Courtney (Brigadier Lethbridge-Stewart)
Spearhead from Space (four parts)
3/1/1970 Part One
10/1/1970 Part Two
17/1/1970 Part Three
24/1/1970 Part Four
Doctor Who and the Silurians (seven parts)
31/1/1970 Part One
7/2/1970 Part Two
14/2/1970 Part Three
21/2/1970 Part Four
28/2/1970 Part Five
7/3/1970 Part Six
14/3/1970 Part Seven
The Ambassadors of Death (seven parts)
21/3/1970 Part One
28/3/1970 Part Two
4/4/1970 Part Three
11/4/1970 Part Four
18/4/1970 Part Five
25/4/1970 Part Six
2/5/1970 Part Seven
Inferno (seven parts)
9/5/1970 Part One
16/5/1970 Part Two
23/5/1970 Part Three
30/5/1970 Part Four
6/6/1970 Part Five
13/6/1970 Part Six
20/6/1970 Part Seven

Series Eight
Regular Cast
Jon Pertwee (The Doctor)
Katy Manning (Jo Grant)
Nicholas Courtney (Brigadier Lethbridge-Stewart)
Roger Delgado (The Master)
Terror of the Autons (four parts)

129

2/1/1971 Part One
9/1/1971 Part Two
16/1/1971 Part Three
23/1/1971 Part Four
The Mind of Evil (six parts)
30/1/1971 Part One
6/2/1971 Part Two
13/2/1971 Part Three
20/2/1971 Part Four
27/2/1971 Part Five
6/3/1971 Part Six
The Claws of Axos (four parts)
13/3/1971 Part One
20/3/1971 Part Two
27/3/1971 Part Three
3/4/1971 Part Four
Colony in Space (six parts)
10/4/1971 Part One
17/4/1971 Part Two
24/4/1971 Part Three
1/5/1971 Part Four
8/5/1971 Part Five
15/5/1971 Part Six
The Dæmons (five parts)
22/5/1971 Part One
29/5/1971 Part Two
5/6/1971 Part Three
12/6/1971 Part Four
19/6/1971 Part Five

Series Nine
Regular Cast
Jon Pertwee (The Doctor)
Katy Manning (Jo Grant)
Roger Delgado (The Master)
Day of the Daleks (four parts)
1/1/1972 Part One
8/1/1972 Part Two
15/1/1972 Part Three
22/1/1972 Part Four
The Curse of Peladon (four parts)
29/1/1972 Part One
5/2/1972 Part Two
12/2/1972 Part Three
19/2/1972 Part Four
The Sea Devils (six parts)
26/2/1972 Part One
4/3/1972 Part Two
11/3/1972 Part Three
18/3/1972 Part Four
25/3/1972 Part Five
1/4/1972 Part Six
The Mutants (six parts)
8/4/1972 Part One

15/4/1972 Part Two
22/4/1972 Part Three
29/4/1972 Part Four
6/5/1972 Part Five
13/5/1972 Part Six
The Time Monster (six parts)
20/5/1972 Part One
27/5/1972 Part Two
3/6/1972 Part Three
10/6/1972 Part Four
17/6/1972 Part Five
24/6/1972 Part Six

Series Ten
Regular Cast
Jon Pertwee (The Doctor)
Katy Manning (Jo Grant)
The Three Doctors (four parts)
30/12/1973 Part One
6/1/1973 Part Two
13/1/1973 Part Three
20/1/1973 Part Four
Carnival of Monsters (four parts)
27/1/1973 Part One
3/2/1973 Part Two
10/2/1973 Part Three
17/2/1973 Part Four
Frontier in Space (six parts)
24/2/1973 Part One
3/3/1973 Part Two
10/3/1973 Part Three
17/3/1973 Part Four
24/3/1973 Part Five
31/3/1973 Part Six
Planet of the Daleks (six parts)
7/4/1973 Part One
14/4/1973 Part Two
21/4/1973 Part Three
28/4/1973 Part Four
5/5/1973 Part Five
12/5/1973 Part Six
The Green Death (six parts)
19/5/1973 Part One
26/5/1973 Part Two
2/6/1973 Part Three
9/6/1973 Part Four
16/6/1973 Part Five
23/6/1973 Part Six

Series Eleven
Regular Cast
Jon Pertwee (The Doctor)

Elisabeth Sladen (Sarah Jane Smith)
Nicholas Courtney (Brigadier Lethbridge-Stewart)
The Time Warrior (four parts)
15/12/1973 Part One
22/12/1973 Part Two
29/12/1973 Part Three
5/1/1974 Part Four
Invasion of the Dinosaurs (six parts)
12/1/1974 Part One
19/1/1974 Part Two
26/1/1974 Part Three
2/2/1974 Part Four
9/2/1974 Part Five
16/2/1974 Part Six
Death to the Daleks (four parts)
23/2/1974 Part One
2/3/1974 Part Two
9/3/1974 Part Three
16/3/1974 Part Four
The Monster of Peladon (six parts)
23/3/1974 Part One
30/3/1974 Part Two
6/4/1974 Part Three
13/4/1974 Part Four
20/4/1974 Part Five
27/4/1974 Part Six
Planet of the Spiders (six parts)
4/5/1974 Part One
11/5/1974 Part Two
18/5/1974 Part Three
25/5/1974 Part Four
1/6/1974 Part Five
8/6/1974 Part Six

Series Twelve
Regular Cast
Tom Baker (The Doctor)
Elisabeth Sladen (Sarah Jane Smith)
Ian Marter (Harry Sullivan)
Robot (four parts)
28/12/1974 Part One
4/1/1975 Part Two
11/1/1975 Part Three
18/1/1975 Part Four
The Ark in Space (four parts)
25/1/1975 Part One
1/2/1975 Part Two

8/2/1975 Part Three
15/2/1975 Part Four
The Sontaran Experiment
(two parts)
22/2/1975 Part One
1/3/1975 Part Two
Genesis of the Daleks (six
parts)
8/3/1975 Part One
15/3/1975 Part Two
22/3/1975 Part Three
29/3/1975 Part Four
5/4/1975 Part Five
12/4/1975 Part Six
Revenge of the Cybermen
(four parts)
19/4/1975 Part One
26/4/1975 Part Two
3/5/1975 Part Three
10/5/1975 Part Four

Series Thirteen

Regular Cast
Tom Baker (The Doctor)
Elisabeth Sladen (Sarah Jane
Smith)
Terror of the Zygons (four
parts)
30/8/1975 Part One
6/9/1975 Part Two
13/9/1975 Part Three
20/9/1975 Part Four
Planet of Evil (four parts)
27/9/1975 Part One
4/10/1975 Part Two
11/10/1975 Part Three
18/10/1975 Part Four
Pyramids of Mars (four parts)
25/10/1975 Part One
1/11/1975 Part Two
8/11/1975 Part Three
15/11/1975 Part Four
The Android Invasion (four
parts)
22/11/1975 Part One
29/11/1975 Part Two
6/12/1975 Part Three
13/12/1975 Part Four
The Brain of Morbius (four
parts)
3/1/1976 Part One
10/1/1976 Part Two
17/1/1976 Part Three
24/1/1976 Part Four
The Seeds of Doom (six parts)

31/1/1976 Part One
7/2/1976 Part Two
14/2/1976 Part Three
21/2/1976 Part Four
28/2/1976 Part Five
6/3/1976 Part Six

Series Fourteen

Regular Cast
Tom Baker (The Doctor)
Louise Jameson (Leela)
The Masque of Mandragora
(four parts)
4/9/1976 Part One
11/9/1976 Part Two
18/9/1976 Part Three
25/9/1976 Part Four
The Hand of Fear (four
parts)
2/10/1976 Part One
9/10/1976 Part Two
16/10/1976 Part Three
23/10/1976 Part Four
The Deadly Assassin (four
parts)
30/10/1976 Part One
6/11/1976 Part Two
13/11/1976 Part Three
20/11/1976 Part Four
The Face of Evil (four parts)
1/1/1977 Part One
8/1/1977 Part Two
15/1/1977 Part Three
22/1/1977 Part Four
The Robots of Death (four
parts)
29/1/1977 Part One
5/2/1977 Part Two
12/2/1977 Part Three
19/2/1977 Part Four
The Talons of Weng-Chiang
(six parts)
26/2/1977 Part One
5/3/1977 Part Two
12/3/1977 Part Three
19/3/1977 Part Four
26/3/1977 Part Five
2/4/1977 Part Six

Series Fifteen

Regular Cast
Tom Baker (The Doctor)
Louise Jameson (Leela)
Horror of Fang Rock (four
parts)

3/9/1977 Part One
10/9/1977 Part Two
17/9/1977 Part Three
24/9/1977 Part Four
The Invisible Enemy (four
parts)
1/10/1977 Part One
8/10/1977 Part Two
15/10/1977 Part Three
22/10/1977 Part Four
Image of the Fendahl (four
parts)
29/10/1977 Part One
5/11/1977 Part Two
12/11/1977 Part Three
19/11/1977 Part Four
The Sun Makers (four parts)
26/11/1977 Part One
3/12/1977 Part Two
10/12/1977 Part Three
17/12/1977 Part Four
Underworld (four parts)
7/1/1978 Part One
14/1/1978 Part Two
21/1/1978 Part Three
28/1/1978 Part Four
The Invasion of Time (six
parts)
4/2/1978 Part One
11/2/1978 Part Two
18/2/1978 Part Three
25/2/1978 Part Four
4/3/1978 Part Five
11/3/1978 Part Six

Series Sixteen

Regular Cast
Tom Baker (The Doctor)
Mary Tamm (Romana)
The Ribos Operation (four
parts)
2/9/1978 Part One
9/9/1978 Part Two
16/9/1978 Part Three
23/9/1978 Part Four
The Pirate Planet (four parts)
30/9/1978 Part One
7/10/1978 Part Two
14/10/1978 Part Three
21/10/1978 Part Four
The Stones of Blood (four
parts)
28/10/1978 Part One
4/11/1978 Part Two
11/11/1978 Part Three

18/11/1978 Part Four
The Androids of Tara (four parts)
25/11/1978 Part One
2/12/1978 Part Two
9/12/1978 Part Three
16/12/1978 Part Four
The Power of Kroll (four parts)
23/12/1978 Part One
30/12/1978 Part Two
6/1/1979 Part Three
13/1/1979 Part Four
The Armageddon Factor (six parts)
20/1/1979 Part One
27/1/1979 Part Two
3/2/1979 Part Three
10/2/1979 Part Four
17/2/1979 Part Five
24/2/1979 Part Six

Series Seventeen
Regular Cast
Tom Baker (The Doctor)
Lalla Ward (Romana)
Destiny of the Daleks (four parts)
1/9/1979 Part One
8/9/1979 Part Two
15/9/1979 Part Three
22/9/1979 Part Four
City of Death (four parts)
29/9/1979 Part One
6/10/1979 Part Two
13/10/1979 Part Three
20/10/1979 Part Four
The Creature from the Pit (four parts)
27/10/1979 Part One
3/11/1979 Part Two
10/11/1979 Part Three
17/11/1979 Part Four
Nightmare of Eden (four parts)
24/11/1979 Part One
1/12/1979 Part Two
8/12/1979 Part Three
15/12/1979 Part Four
The Horns of Nimon (four parts)
22/12/1979 Part One
29/12/1979 Part Two
5/1/1980 Part Three
12/1/1980 Part Four
Shada (six parts)
(not aired)

Series Eighteen
Regular Cast
Tom Baker (The Doctor)
Lalla Ward (Romana)
Matthew Waterhouse (Adric)
John Leeson (voice of K9)
The Leisure Hive (four parts)
30/8/1980 Part One
6/9/1980 Part Two
13/9/1980 Part Three
20/9/1980 Part Four
Meglos (four parts)
27/9/1980 Part One
4/10/1980 Part Two
11/10/1980 Part Three
18/10/1980 Part Four
Full Circle (four parts)
25/10/1980 Part One
1/11/1980 Part Two
8/11/1980 Part Three
15/11/1980 Part Four
State of Decay (four parts)
22/11/1980 Part One
29/11/1980 Part Two
6/12/1980 Part Three
13/12/1980 Part Four
Warriors' Gate (four parts)
3/1/1981 Part One
10/1/1981 Part Two
17/1/1981 Part Three
24/1/1981 Part Four
The Keeper of Traken (four parts)
31/1/1981 Part One
7/2/1981 Part Two
14/2/1981 Part Three
21/2/1981 Part Four
Logopolis (four parts)
28/2/1981 Part One
7/3/1981 Part Two
14/3/1981 Part Three
21/3/1981 Part Four

Series Nineteen
Regular Cast
Tom Baker (The Doctor)
Matthew Waterhouse (Adric)
Janet Fielding (Tegan)
Sarah Sutton (Nyssa)
Castrovalva (four parts)
4/1/1982 Part One
5/1/1982 Part Two
11/1/1982 Part Three
12/1/1982 Part Four

Four to Doomsday (four parts)
18/1/1982 Part One
19/1/1982 Part Two
25/1/1982 Part Three
26/1/1982 Part Four
Kinda (four parts)
1/2/1982 Part One
2/2/1982 Part Two
8/2/1982 Part Three
9/2/1982 Part Four
The Visitation (four parts)
15/2/1982 Part One
16/2/1982 Part Two
22/2/1982 Part Three
23/2/1982 Part Four
Black Orchid (two parts)
1/3/1982 Part One
2/3/1982 Part Two
Earthshock (four parts)
8/3/1982 Part One
9/3/1982 Part Two
15/3/1982 Part Three
16/3/1982 Part Four
Time-Flight (four parts)
22/3/1982 Part One
23/3/1982 Part Two
29/3/1982 Part Three
30/3/1982 Part Four

Series Twenty
Regular Cast
Peter Davison (The Doctor)
Janet Fielding (Tegan)
Sarah Sutton (Nyssa)
Mark Strickson (Turlough)
Arc of Infinity (four parts)
3/1/1983 Part One
5/1/1983 Part Two
11/1/1983 Part Three
12/1/1983 Part Four
Snakedance (four parts)
18/1/1983 Part One
19/1/1983 Part Two
25/1/1983 Part Three
26/1/1983 Part Four
Mawdryn Undead (four parts)
1/2/1983 Part One
2/2/1983 Part Two
8/2/1983 Part Three
9/2/1983 Part Four
Terminus (four parts)
15/2/1983 Part One
16/2/1983 Part Two
22/2/1983 Part Three

23/2/1983 Part Four
Enlightenment (four parts)
1/3/1983 Part One
2/3/1983 Part Two
8/3/1983 Part Three
9/3/1983 Part Four
The King's Demons (two parts)
15/3/1983 Part One
16/3/1983 Part Two

Series Twenty One
Regular Cast
Peter Davison/Colin Baker (The Doctor)
Janet Fielding (Tegan)
Nicola Bryant (Peri)
Warriors of the Deep (four parts)
5/1/1984 Part One
6/1/1984 Part Two
12/1/1984 Part Three
13/1/1984 Part Four
The Awakening (two parts)
19/1/1984 Part One
20/1/1984 Part Two
Frontios (four parts)
26/1/1984 Part One
27/1/1984 Part Two
2/2/1984 Part Three
3/2/1984 Part Four
Resurrection of the Daleks (two parts)
8/2/1984 Part One (45m)
15/2/1984 Part Two (45m)
Planet of Fire (four parts)
23/2/1984 Part One
24/2/1984 Part Two
1/3/1984 Part Three
2/3/1984 Part Four
The Caves of Androzani (four parts)
8/3/1984 Part One
9/3/1984 Part Two
15/3/1984 Part Three
16/3/1984 Part Four
The Twin Dilemma (four parts)
22/3/1984 Part One
23/3/1984 Part Two
29/3/1984 Part Three
30/3/1984 Part Four

Series Twenty Two
Regular Cast
Colin Baker (The Doctor)
Nicola Bryant (Peri)
Attack of the Cybermen (two parts)
5/1/1985 Part One
12/1/1985 Part Two
Vengeance on Varos (two parts)
19/1/1985 Part One
26/1/1985 Part Two
The Mark of the Rani (two parts)
2/2/1985 Part One
9/2/1985 Part Two
The Two Doctors (three parts)
16/2/1985 Part One
23/2/1985 Part Two
2/3/1985 Part Three
Timelash (two parts)
9/3/1985 Part One
16/3/1985 Part Two
Revelation of the Daleks (two parts)
23/3/1985 Part One
30/3/1985 Part Two

Series Twenty Three
Regular Cast
Colin Baker (The Doctor)
Bonnie Langford (Mel)
Michael Jayston (The Valeyard)
Lynda Bellingham (The Inquisitor)
The Trial of a Time Lord (fourteen parts in all, divided into four stories)
The Mysterious Planet
6/9/1986 Part One
13/9/1986 Part Two
20/9/1986 Part Three
27/9/1986 Part Four
Mindwarp
4/10/1986 Part One
11/10/1986 Part Two
18/10/1986 Part Three
25/10/1986 Part Four
Terror of the Vervoids
1/11/1986 Part One
8/11/1986 Part Two
15/11/1986 Part Three
22/11/1986 Part Four

The Ultimate Foe
29/11/1986 Part One
6/12/1986 Part Two

Series Twenty Four
Regular Cast
Colin Baker (The Doctor)
Bonnie Langford (Mel)
Time and the Rani (four parts)
7/9/1987 Part One
14/9/1987 Part Two
21/9/1987 Part Three
28/9/1987 Part Four
Paradise Towers (four parts)
5/10/1987 Part One
12/10/1987 Part Two
19/10/1987 Part Three
26/10/1987 Part Four
Delta and the Bannermen (three parts)
2/11/1987 Part One
9/11/1987 Part Two
16/11/1987 Part Three
Dragonfire (three parts)
23/11/1987 Part One
30/11/1987 Part Two
7/12/1987 Part Three

Series Twenty Five
Regular Cast
Sylvester McCoy (The Doctor)
Sophie Aldred (Ace)
Remembrance of the Daleks (four parts)
5/10/1988 Part One
12/10/1988 Part Two
19/10/1988 Part Three
26/10/1988 Part Four
The Happiness Patrol (three parts)
2/11/1988 Part One
9/11/1988 Part Two
16/11/1988 Part Three
Silver Nemesis (three parts)
23/11/1988 Part One
30/11/1988 Part Two
7/12/1988 Part Three
The Greatest Show in the Galaxy (four parts)
14/12/1988 Part One
21/12/1988 Part Two
28/12/1988 Part Three
4/1/1989 Part Four

Series Twenty Six
Regular Cast
Sylvester McCoy (The Doctor)
Sophie Aldred (Ace)
Battlefield (four parts)
6/9/1989 Part One
13/9/1989 Part Two
20/9/1989 Part Three
27/9/1989 Part Four
Ghost Light (three parts)
4/10/1989 Part One
11/10/1989 Part Two
18/10/1989 Part Three
The Curse of Fenric (four parts)
25/10/1989 Part One
1/11/1989 Part Two
8/11/1989 Part Three
15/11/1989 Part Four
Survival (three parts)
22/11/1989 Part One
29/11/1989 Part Two
6/12/1989 Part Three

2005 New Series One
Regular Cast
Christopher Eccleston (The Doctor)
Billie Piper (Rose Tyler)
Camille Coduri (Jackie Tyler)
Noel Clarke (Mickey Smith)
26/03/2005 Rose
2/04/2005 The End of the World
9/04/2005 The Unquiet Dead
16/04/2005 Aliens of London
23/04/2005 World War Three
30/04/2005 Dalek
7/05/2005 The Long Game
14/05/2005 Father's Day
21/05/2005 The Empty Child
28/05/2005 The Doctor Dances
4/06/2005 Boom Town
11/06/2005 Bad Wolf
18/06/2005 The Parting of the Ways

TV Film
Doctor Who
US 14/05/1996
UK 27/05/1996 (US/UK) (1 x 84m)
Main Cast
Paul McGann (The Doctor)
Eric Roberts (The Master)
Sylvester McCoy (The Old Doctor)

Specials
25/11/1983 *The Five Doctors* (1 x 90m)
Main Cast
Peter Davison (The Fifth Doctor)
Jon Pertwee (The Third Doctor)
Patrick Troughton (The Second Doctor)
Richard Hurndall (The First Doctor)
26–27/11/1993 'Dimensions in Time' (2 x 7m, for Children in Need)
Main Cast
Jon Pertwee (The Third Doctor)
Tom Baker (The Fourth Doctor)
Peter Davison (The Fifth Doctor)
Colin Baker (The Sixth Doctor)
Sylvester McCoy (The Seventh Doctor)
12/03/1999 'Doctor Who and the Curse of Fatal Death' (four parts, for Red Nose Day)
Cast
Rowan Atkinson (The Doctor)
Jonathan Pryce (The Master)
Julia Sawalha (Emma)

Index

Page numbers in *italics* indicate illustrations.

135

137